CELEBRATION
OF HAND-HOOKED
RUGS 27
2017 Edition

Editor
Debra Smith

Celebration Coordinator
Jessica Thelander

Designer
CW Design Solutions, Inc.

Advertising Director
Keith Kousins

Advertising Coordinator
Jenny Latwesen

Customer Service
Publisher's Service Associates
U.S. (877) 297-0965
Canada (866) 375-8626

Publisher
Ampry Publishing, LLC

*Rug photographs provided by the artists
unless otherwise noted.*

Rug Hooking (ISSN 1045-4373) is
published five times a year in Jan./Feb.,
March/April/May, June/July/Aug.,Sept./
Oct., and Nov./Dec. by Ampry Publish-
ing, LLC, 3400 Dundee Road, Suite 220,
Northbrook, IL 60062. *Celebration of
Hand-Hooked Rugs* is published annually.

Contents Copyright© 2017. All rights reserv-
ed. Reproduction in whole or part without
the written consent of the publisher is
prohibited. Canadian GST #R137954772.

NOTICE: All patterns and hooked pieces
presented here are Copyright© the individual designers, who are named in the
corresponding captions. No hooked piece
presented here may be duplicated in any
form without the designer's consent.

A Publication of

R·U·G
HOOKING

P.O. Box 388
Shermans Dale, PA 17090

www.rughookingmagazine.com
rughook@amprycp.com
ISBN-978-1-945550-08-9

Printed in U.S.A.

WELCOME TO CELEBR

Why do we hook?

We are pleased to present to you the latest edition of *Celebration of Hand-Hooked Rugs*. Sit back and enjoy the creativity, the imagination, and the stellar technique shown in these hooked pieces. Immerse yourself in these pages and consider the artists who hook them and why they hook.

As we prepare to put this book together each spring, we ask the Celebration finalists about their rugs and their process. The answers we get are always interesting, sometimes curious or humorous, and occasionally thought provoking. The finalists in Celebration 27 had a resounding response to our question, "Why do you hook rugs?" Time and time again the rug hookers commented on the calming effect of our fiber art. It was a recurring theme, stated over and over again:

I enjoy the meditative space I get into when I hook… rug hooking is "wool therapy"… It's relaxing, almost meditative… It's the process that keeps me coming back for more… Rug hooking is my sanity… I couldn't wait to get my own tools: the stripper, the frame, and a hook. I knew I needed to do this… It's the creative and meditative outlet that helps me keep a balanced life…

You know what they are talking about: loop after loop after loop; the rhythmic, repetitive movement that calms and soothes. You may have seen the recent studies addressing the benefits of crafts, the studies that have found that using our hands to create, especially in the fiber arts, is indeed good for us. Arts and crafts are relaxing, meditative, stimulating to the brain and imagination. Hooking is good for the heart, good for the soul, and good for our peace of mind. Not only are we healthier and happier, we have a fabulous piece of art that we can be proud of. As one of our finalists put it: *The world may be a mess, but my big concern is how does that color work with what is next to it?*

That about sums it up, doesn't it? Rug hooking can be an aid to mental health and emotional well-being—a prescription for whatever ails us. So go find a hook, a piece of linen, a great design, and get hooking!

Debra Smith, *Editor*
Jessica Thelander, *Celebration Coordinator*

READERS' CHOICE
Remember to vote for your favorite rugs. All voting will be online this year and it is easy to do: just go to www. rughookingmagazine.com, tap or click on Celebration Readers' Choice and tell us which rugs you like the best. The results will be published in the June/July/August 2018 issue. We look forward to getting your vote!

ON THE COVER

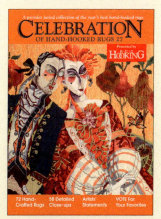

THE CONSPIRACY,
hooked by Marion Sachs. See the
full rug on page 91.

Table of Contents

RUGS BASED ON ORIGINAL DESIGNS

RUGS BASED ON COMMERCIAL DESIGNS

RUGS BASED ON ADAPTATIONS

RUGS BASED ON PRIMITIVE DESIGNS

HONORABLE MENTIONS

Meet the Judges

Each year a new panel of judges takes on the daunting task of evaluating Celebration entries. Imagine the enormity of this task: each entry comes with 4 separate photos, so in a field of 170 entries, the judges will review and evaluate a total of 680 photographs. Quite an undertaking: it is an enormous commitment of time and energy. Hours and hours of concentration, deliberation, and careful consideration; the judges essentially commit one week in early January to Celebration judging. All for the love of rug hooking.

We are pleased that each year we have such talented people willing to act as judges. It is their expertise and wide-ranging experience that makes *Celebration* work so well; they are the foundation of the whole enterprise.

And so we extend our heartfelt thanks to these four women and to all the judges who have gone before. If you have the opportunity, be sure to thank a judge. Their contributions cannot be overstated.

GAIL BECKER

Gail has been rug hooking for almost 20 years and credits Nancy Miller Quigley for teaching her the technical and finer points of the craft. Nancy encouraged Gail to attend as many camps as she could and sponsored her for Western McGown Teacher's Workshop, where she was certified in 2003. Gail teaches at her home studio and at camps and workshops in the U.S. and Canada, where she enjoys collaborating with her students.

One of Gail's most rewarding accomplishments was to create the blog, Postcards from California, Fiber Art Challenge. The hooked postcard-sized mats that she received were assembled into a traveling display that Gail took to the ATHA Biennial in Long Beach and many camps and guilds where she spoke about the artists and the California memories that inspired their postcards. The postcards were featured in Rug Beat and an article in *RHM*.

Gail continues to write articles for *ATHA Art of Rug Hooking* and has been an Associate Editor there since 2010. She serves as ATHA Region 12 representative, where she created a website for members to communicate. Gail continues her own rug hooking education by attending camps and through her activities in several guilds.

PEGGY HANNUM

As a McGown Certified Instructor, Peggy taught for 19 years in Lancaster and at rug schools in the U.S. and Canada. She retired from teaching and from her role as historian for the McGown Guild in 2015 and is enjoying traveling with her husband to visit her New England children and grandchildren.

Peggy and her husband continue to travel overseas, leading a group (half of them her hooking students!) to Israel and Palestine where they served as liaisons for the United Methodist Church. After downsizing and moving, Peggy is finally getting back to some serious hooking.

Peggy continues to emulate her teachers and mentors: Meredith

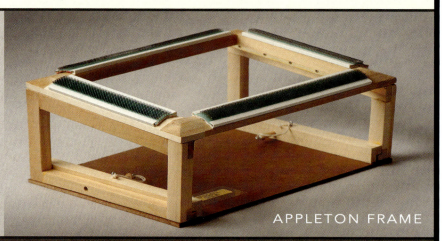

LeBeau and Nancy Blood. Her rugs were featured in nine past *Celebration* editions, including the very first *Celebration*, and her rug was on the cover of *Celebration 25*. Peggy has had many award-winning rugs selected for the annual Gallery Show of the Pennsylvania Guild of Craftsmen. Peggy continues to maintain her website, *www.peggyhannum.com*, adding rugs and published articles.

DIANE STOFFEL

Diane started rug hooking in the 1970s. After meeting Maryanne Lincoln, she joined the McGown guild and the just-forming ATHA. She began teaching in 1980 and currently travels to teach at many camps and private groups each year.

Diane loves all aspects of rug hooking: drawing, color planning, dyeing, and working with students to help them make their rugs the best possible. She appreciates all styles of rug hooking, and with an art background, she is able to apply that knowledge to her own work and to help the students in her classes achieve their goals.

Diane is pleased that many of the rugs that she has taught have appeared in *Celebration* and *Rug Hooking* magazine.

MICHELE WISE

Artist, teacher, and life-long learner, Michele has been hooking for 18 years, and has taught rug hooking across the U.S. and internationally. She looks for opportunities to expand the possibilities of this textile medium to introduce it to more and more people wherever she goes. In her mind, the potential for creativity in rug hooking is endless and Michele loves that about her chosen craft.

Michele promotes rug hooking by encouraging memberships in ATHA, TIGHR, National Guild of Pearl K. McGown, and guilds in Australia. She is the director of the McGown Western Teacher's Workshop, co-director of Puget Sound Rug School, and the director of the Reiter Retreats.

Michele has written articles for *Rug Hooking* magazine, *ATHA Art of Rug Hooking*, *Wool Street Journal*, *Rug Beat*, *TIGHR*, The Aussie Rug Making Guild, and the Pearl McGown Guild. Her rugs appear in many published books. She has won awards for her rugs at GMRG in Vermont, local and state fairs, fiber events, and in *Celebration*. Two of her pieces are on permanent display at Bainbridge Art Museum on Bainbridge Island, Washington.

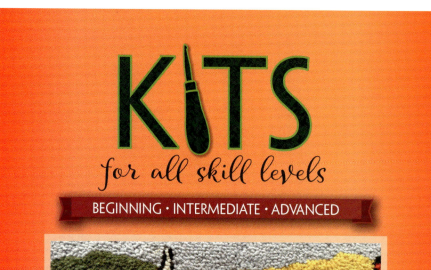

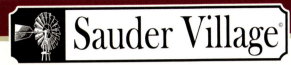

Afterlife

Inspiration for this rug came from studying the embroidered cloths of the Kuba tribe from what used to be the Congo. These intricate patterns were done from the 1600s until about 1950 and were often used as ceremonial dress, as currency, and death shrouds. I would take a few of the motifs and fit them to the square grid of the hooking foundation.

The Kuba also had limited color choices due to the scarce dye sources of the Congo region. You'd usually see black and a dirty orange color in most of their graphic designs. I tried to use these and some complementary colors to enhance the design. There are two sections that I love in the piece. The first is the two flaring orange motifs that make up the upper portion of the rug, and the second is the colored triangles that flow through the middle.

Connecting the two ends in the middle was the most challenging since I needed to find a way to complete both sections. I didn't draw anything on the backing; I just free hooked to see what would happen. I had the expert input of Stephanie Krauss of Green Mountain Hooked Rugs to advise me to introduce calmer colors to help blend the whole thing. My tendency is to use brighter colors with a lot more punch, so this was a different approach for me. I trusted her instinct, put the hook to the backing, and began, and I'm pleased with how it turned out. Since I'm terrible at sewing, I had Ann French finish the rug for me.

I can remember the first time I got into rug hooking. It was about 1999 on a drive around Lake Sunapee in New Hampshire that I saw a sign at an old inn that said "Hook-in Today." I pulled in and saw a room full of people making the most amazing rugs I'd ever seen. I came away thinking that I could do that too. It's a short drive from there to the Dorr Mill Store, so off I went and bought a pillow pattern, a primitive frame (with thumbtacks holding on the backing), and a small hook. There are so many reasons why I enjoy hooking rugs, like the materials and the studio where I work. And truthfully, I really enjoy the meditative space you get into when you hook. The world may be in chaos, but at the moment, my big concern is "how does that color work with what's next to it."

Edward O'Keeffe
East Thetford, Vermont

Ed sells high-end handmade furniture in his shop in Vermont and custom pieces for people all over the country. He's a self-taught rug hooker and is a member of the Green Mountain Rug Hooking Guild. This is his first appearance in Celebration.

In The Judges' Eyes

Excellent shading to illustrate theme; has a look of Klimt straight lines; enjoy the red-violet accents; the harmonious color plan enhances the design; a smart use of textured wool.

Afterlife, 23½" x 53", #4-, #5- and #7-cut hand-dyed wool on linen.
Designed and hooked by Ed O'Keeffe, East Thetford, Vermont, 2016.

Antique Shop Canning Jars

Wherever I go, I'm always on the lookout for interesting objects to use in still life compositions for my hookings. An array of old bottles and canning jars was spotted tucked away in a corner of an antique shop that my husband, Jim, and I browsed through on one of our regular trips to North Carolina's Outer Banks. It was the perfect subject. The shelf was lined with red paper, and a window, just a bit behind, made for the most fantastic reflections and colors with plenty of reds, blues, rusty browns, and white, which is a color palette I've used in almost all of my hookings. The window cast its image on the middle jar, and bottles were reflected in and through other jars. The biggest attraction was the raised lettering on the jars. This was an exciting new challenge. I couldn't wait to get started.

All of the wool used in this piece was wool I already had in my stash or had previously dyed. It was a good use for a lot of my cut strips left over from other hookings.

I attacked this composition from the darkest jar to the lightest, working first on the lettering, putting in the highlights and then the dark shadows of each individual letter, treating each as an entity of its own. I'm really thrilled with the way the brand name lettering on the jars came out, even when the jars are turned away from the viewer. Hooking the rest of the piece was much the same. I always put in the highlights and darkest shades first, paying attention to the shapes and placement of color masses. I did find a bit of a difficulty in hooking the wire clamps used to seal the old jars. In order to make some parts seem to overlap others, I had to interrupt the hooking of the underneath wires with a darker shade of wire, which then appears to go over them.

The very best part of this hooking, though, is the memories it evokes of growing up in Vermont, watching my mother and grandmothers can fruits and vegetables every fall. We stored these canned goods in our cellars and used them all winter long. I can still see the shelves full of canned peaches and blackberries (my favorites).

Antique Shop Canning Jars won Grand Champion and Best in Show at the Montgomery County Agricultural Fair in Maryland in 2016, was exhibited at The Columbia Center for the Arts in Maryland in March 2016, and appeared in the January/February 2017 issue of *Rug Hooking* magazine.

Antique Shop Canning Jars, 23" x 16", #3-cut as-is and hand-dyed wool on linen. Designed and hooked by Carol Koerner, Bethesda, Maryland, 2016.

Carol Koerner
Bethesda, Maryland

Carol is a member of ATHA, has participated in many hooking exhibits, has won numerous ribbons for her work, has written articles for Rug Hooking magazine, and volunteers and judges every summer at her county fair. This is her thirteenth appearance in Celebration.

In The Judges' Eyes

Blocks of color create great jewel effect of glass; the red background nicely frames the composition. Displays a clear understanding of iridescence of glass, especially impressive lettering.

Autumn's Beauty

Autumn's Beauty is a symphony of change. It reveals the exquisite elements of nature. Late September, on an island in beautiful Northern Ontario, the autumn sunshine and change of season painted a rich and vibrant mosaic of colors that fluttered in the autumn air. It was a pristine moment I felt compelled to capture. I feel that my artistic skills enhanced my ability to take this medium from the floor to a unique piece of fine art wall hanging. We live in such a colorful world that this piece was the perfect inspirational trigger.

Visually, there is always an element of surprise when creating on a flat surface with woolen fibers. The materials I picked mingle and interact in a unique way, enhancing my piece with the element of realism. My color palette is always changing. Processing the visual information of the beautiful fall colors lent an intriguing color play to my piece. I created the colors through a dye process by eye and discovered a world of opportunity to use colors in a fresh way.

I loved creating the leaves the most. Each leaf was a composition within the larger composition. The autumn breeze was the most challenging to capture. I needed to create an unseen yet present element, which was reflected in the gently created ripples in the water. Art is not just a surface; it is working through ideas that aren't yet realized until I create them and make them come to life.

I first got started in rug hooking when my mother-in-law gave me a wall hanging that she had hooked. It was a new visual medium for me, and it sparked my interest. I have had a love of the arts for years and have created pieces in many mediums. I love the whole process of rug hooking and all the skills it takes to create each piece.

Autumn's Beauty has appeared in the Muskoka Arts & Crafts Incorporated 39th Spring Members' Show, where it won the Award of Excellence for Fibre Arts. I was also a featured artist at the Ontario Hooking Craft Guild 50th Annual Conference where this piece was an honorable mention in the "Originals" category.

Diane Ayles
Huntsville, Ontario, Canada

Diane is a professional artist and belongs to the Ontario Hooking Craft Guild. She won the Canadian Rug Hooker of the Year Award in 2015 from the Hooked Rug Museum of North America. This is her fifth appearance in Celebration.

In The Judges' Eyes

Wonderful ripple effect on the water; excellent play of light and shadows; the water sparkles; warm and cool colors promote dimensionality.

Autumn's Beauty, 37½" x 24¾", #1- to 3-cut hand-dyed, vintage, textured, and plaid wool with a touch of satin on linen. Designed and hooked by Diane Ayles, Huntsville, Ontario, Canada, 2015.

Badland Survivor

I've been in love with the tree I featured in this rug since childhood. I grew up on a ranch in western North Dakota, and one of my favorite family outings was to go with friends for a picnic to a site west of our ranch in the Badlands. The location was called the burning coal vein, which was where a seam of lignite coal was burning underground, leaving gaping holes where you could see the fire like a furnace. (The exciting part was that you could cook hot dogs on a long stick or hold a steak on a shovel in the fire!) We kids loved to run around the nearby hills and ravines, especially one spot with giant stone concentrations that were great for climbing.

The tree that was my inspiration for this rug grew near these rocks. Even as a child,

I was impressed with that tree. It looked so old, so big, and so different from the nearby juniper trees. We knew it was old since early ranchers in the area observed this same "old tree." I marveled that it apparently had survived all manner of stress. Drought, storms, lightning, and fire had left their marks, but the tree continued to live. Two years ago, I wondered if the tree was still alive. I hadn't been back to the site for 50 years, so I went to see, and there it was, still alive!

I chose colors that you would naturally see in the local vegetation and soil. I did use some violet, magenta, and burgundy for tree shadows. I thought it was more lively and interesting than just dark green.

I was working on the sky at the Prairie

Rose Rug Camp where I could look out big windows at the interaction between the prairie and the sky, but the sky wasn't "cooperating." It was too flat, so I finally stopped looking at the sky in front of me, ripped out what I had done, and drew on my memory bank of colors. I learned that if something doesn't feel or look right, rip it out and try again. The second attempt might be better.

I was first introduced to rug hooking when my friend bought a kit at a quilt show. She let me work on it, and I discovered I rather liked doing it. I refer to rug hooking as "wool therapy." I find the process relaxing. Plus, since I like to use recycled wool, it's a pleasure to reuse something old to make something new to be enjoyed.

Carolyn Godfread
Bismarck, North Dakota

Carolyn has a PhD in botany and most recently worked for a consulting company doing botanical surveys for the oil business in western North Dakota. This is her second appearance in Celebration.

In The Judges' Eyes

Color and forward motion of clouds and trees speak of impending danger; creates a mood of isolation set against the beauty of nature.

Badland Survivor, 37" x 25", #7 and 8- hand-cut dyed and as-is wool on linen.
Designed and hooked by Carolyn Godfread, Bismarck, North Dakota, 2016.

Bulgarian Rose

My husband and I took a Danube River cruise to celebrate our 25th anniversary. On our actual anniversary, April 1st, the ship stopped in Bulgaria. We were taken on a day trip through the countryside where we became aware of the use of roses in everything from cosmetics to cuisine. Big red roses were particularly popular. After we returned home, I decided to make this rug to commemorate the experience.

I dyed Dorr natural wool for the rose and used a multi-fiber yarn for the background in colors that I thought enhanced the rose. Hooking this background with the yarn was challenging for me. The yarn has a shiny surface, which added to the challenge of maintaining uniform loop height (or trying to!). I generally do not enjoy hooking with yarn and so avoid it, but the colors of the yarn used seemed to bring out the red in the rose. The "heart" of the rose is my favorite part of the rug—it stands out to me every time I look at it.

I dyed with Majic Carpet dyes, using a Sarah Ladd formula called "Heart's Red." I chose the color because it was particularly brilliant. It was a 16-swatch set, which was as high as I've ever gone before. Typically, I'll only use 6- or 8-value swatches.

I had always "judged" mock shading to be inferior to finger shading before I hooked this rug. However, the use of mock shading in this rug enhanced the result and taught me to consider this technique in a new light.

I first got started in rug hooking in 1999. My family took a road trip through Quebec. While driving along the south shore of the St. Laurence River, we stopped at a gas station, and the woman at the till had a pile of mats for sale for $25 each. I navigated making a purchase in French and brought home a mat which I then looked at closely

to see how it had been made. That led to a trip to our local library where I borrowed an old book describing hooking techniques. One large embroidery hoop, a crochet hook, and some hand-cut wool fabric later, and I was off to the races. I love rug hooking

because of its meditative effect after a long day at work, plus I've made many good friends in the hooking community and have enjoyed picking up a little bit of knowledge about color and composition along the way.

Myra Bielby
Edmonton, Alberta, Canada

Myra is an appellate court judge. She is a member of the Edmonton Traditional Rug Hookers and the Prairie Harvest Rug Hooking School. This is her second appearance in Celebration.

In The Judges' Eyes

Textured background enhances the deceptively simple design; mock shading at its finest; lovely depth of shading in rose; nice asymmetrical composition; value steps make the rose appear lifelike.

Bulgarian Rose, 20½" x 14½", #4-cut hand-dyed wool and multi-composition yarn on linen. Designed and hooked by Myra Bielby, Edmonton, Alberta, Canada, 2015.

Cinder

I hooked this rug of my daughter's cat, Cinder, from a photograph I took of him. I loved the pose he was in because it shows his attitude towards life. Cats have a special way of making life all about them. Although he is mostly very laid back, he expects to be waited on and pampered at all times.

I wanted to create black by using other colors like purples and dark blues. They helped to make the piece look more realistic and not just a black blob. I hand-dye almost all of my wool and like to experiment with colors.

I had a fun time hooking this rug, starting from designing the piece with the photo to hand dyeing the colors and finally pulling that last stitch. He was originally on a flat beige couch, but I put him on the old couch that we had for many years in our living room. It was a challenge to get the fabric to look just right. When hooking this particular section, I learned that less is more!

His pose was also a challenge with his paw coming out from his body creating a skewed look. I hooked him in using mostly directional hooking and did the rest in a more random loop method. I also wanted to include his name but not make it the central focus. It sometimes takes people a few minutes to see his name in the background. To finish the rug, I whipped the edges in wool using a herringbone stitch. I'm so thankful to Donna Hrkman, the Wednesday group, and everyone who helped me along the way in making this rug.

A friend first got me into rug hooking, and it's been a craft I've now enjoyed for years. I love rug hooking because I can start with a blank canvas and white wool and end up with a beautiful work of art through designing and dyeing. I have hooked for over 15 years and am a certified McGown instructor. I recently spent a month in Iceland as an artist in residence and loved it. While I dabble in almost all fiber arts, rug hooking is my favorite.

Laurie Wiles
Edmonton, Alberta, Canada

Laurie is an artist who has won several awards in different juried shows. She's a member of the Edmonton Rug Hooking Guild, TIGHR, ATHA, Western McGown teachers, and PHRHSA.

In The Judges' Eyes

Exquisite composition; shadows and highlights add to the drama of this piece; chair pattern adds subtle repetition to the design.

Cinder, 28" x 22", #3- to 5-cut hand-dyed wool on linen.
Designed and hooked by Laurie Wiles, Edmonton, Alberta, Canada, 2014.

Clarkson

My husband, Mark, and I own and operate Twin Lakes Dairy (a Jersey dairy farm), Happy Cattle Company (Angus and Hereford genetics), and Happy Cattle Beef (grass-fed beef). This rug was modeled after my husband's favorite bull in our Angus herd.

Gail Dufresne helped me start the project at the Tyler Star of Texas Rug Camp. She dyed the wool for the beautiful sky and had fuzzy boucle and mohair for the grass. My favorite part of the rug is the bull's head. I started hooking the piece on the rear quarter (left side) of the bull and worked towards his head (right side). I was very concerned about the shading of the bull because I wanted it to look realistic and show his shape.

I was fortunate to meet April DeConick while hooking *Clarkson*. She told me to not be afraid to add more color to the black Angus bull. As a result, I added some blue and purple to his head and brown to his body. It's nowhere near the color variety that April uses in her piece, but it's one more step in the right direction for me.

My husband helped select the frame for *Clarkson*. We have a wonderful local framer that framed the Hereford bull I hooked (shown in *Celebration XXIV*), plus tons of cross-stitch projects, so we knew just who to go to. Both pieces are hanging in our farmhouse office. When people come to purchase Angus and Hereford cattle from us, Mark always shows them these two framed rugs.

I first learned about rug hooking about eight years ago when I met Katie Hartner at a punch needle class in Mineola, Texas. I discovered she had a shop called A Nimble Thimble where I went to purchase wool to use as the background on my framed punch needle pieces. That was the first time I had ever seen hooked rugs. I was in awe at the ones she had hanging in her shop. I signed up for a beginner's class right away.

I love rug hooking because I find it to be more creative than other fiber arts. I love the colors and textures and how fast a rug hooking project can be completed. I enjoy the range of cuts and fabrics and using patterns along with designing my own. You can make a rug for the floor, for hanging, or even make it into a pillow or purse. The possibilities are endless.

Clarkson, 26" x 21", #3- to 6-cut hand-dyed and as-is wool on linen.
Designed and hooked by Laurie Hannan, Athens, Texas, 2016. JAMES ROBERTSON

Laurie Hannan
Athens, Texas

Laurie owns dairy and beef businesses with her husband. She is a member of ATHA and had a landscape rug of hers appear in an ATHA magazine. This is her second appearance in Celebration.

In The Judges' Eyes

The superb hooking technique of the grass and animal make this piece stand out; fine rendering of subject matter.

Dahlia

I was inspired to make this piece as I was walking to the beach in Maine and discovered a wonderful dahlia garden. The colors were spectacular, and I decided I would do a color study by dyeing swatches and doing spot dyes and dip dyes to create this lovely piece.

I so enjoy working with color and wanted to create the many shades and values in the original dahlia flower I photographed. Getting the wonderful sunlight effect on the flower took many different values. I used dip-dyed wool, spot-dyed wool, and 15 gradations of swatches. I love the depth of this flower, particularly with the center portion that seems to pop forward. This piece has made me excited to experiment with more bright colors.

This rug was done using only #3-cut wool. It was my way of blending all the different values, dip dyes, and spot dyes. Dyeing wool is a passion of mine. I love being able to create spectacular colors and see how they play off one another in a finished piece. The background is all done, including the leaves, from one spot-dye piece. The specialty stitches in the border settle and finish this piece nicely, which works well for a wall hanging.

I first got involved in rug hooking in 2003 when my sister-in-law invited me to attend a local hook-in with her. Needless to say, I was "hooked" from the start. I love rug hooking because I enjoy creating my own patterns and love dyeing wool to get the right colors that define me. Along with

being a business manager, I am an artist, designer, teacher, and lover of nature. Rug hooking allows me to express all of my passions in a creative outlet. I especially like sharing my knowledge of rug hooking and dyeing wool with others. I teach at my studio, Vermont Floorcloths and Fiber Arts, here in Cabot, Vermont, where I sell my original-design patterns and hand-dyed wool. It's where I create hand-painted canvas rugs from small runners to room-sized pieces. I also travel to teach groups and get to connect with rug hooking enthusiasts all over the country.

Dahlia, 18" x 19", #3-cut hand-dyed wool in 8 values, dip-dyed and spot-dyed on linen.
Designed and hooked by Sandy Ducharme, Marshfield, Vermont, 2016. BRIAN KLOCKE

Sandy Ducharme
Marshfield, Vermont

Sandy belongs to the Northeast Kingdom Rug Hooking Guild, Green Mountain Rug Hooking Guild, Vermont Craft Council, and Artisans Hand Craft Gallery. She has won "Best of Show" at state fairs three times. This is her third appearance in Celebration.

In The Judges' Eyes

Beautiful; nice branding of hues and values; high contrast makes for a dramatic composition.

Daki-Gashiwa
(Embracing Oak Leaves)

My family crest is called Daki-Gashiwa, meaning "embracing oak leaves." Many of my childhood memories are entwined with it. Every New Year, individual footed lacquer trays, soup bowls, and plates, all embossed with gold Daki-Gashiwa, were brought out from storage, and we would have our New Year's breakfast in the living room. During World War II when we evacuated from air raids to our ancestral village, I spotted my grandmother holding a lighted paper lantern painted with Daki-Gashiwa on the darkened train platform. Despite our reduced circumstances, my mother somehow obtained a quantity of early rayon white fabric and tie-dyed Daki-Gashiwa in the center of the purple futon cover. Although I was very young, I was impressed that my mother could make such a beautiful thing in the makeshift kitchen.

When I visited my family in Japan about seven years ago, my sister-in-law gave me a cotton purple *furoshiki*, dyed out in white with Daki-Gashiwa. It was large, and I thought I could trace it and hook it in the center of a rug. Because the leaves in the crest are stylized, I wanted it surrounded by more realistic oak leaves. I collected oak leaves at our cottage ground and traced them to make the cardboard patterns.

I wanted the rug to have a certain thickness and planned to hook it in a Newfoundland zigzag fashion I learned at Deanne Fitzpatrick's workshop about 10 years ago. I hooked the body of the rug in #8-cut wool in a zigzag, outlined in straight traditional hooking in a #6 cut. Since the zigzag part would be pulled up high,

about ½", and the outlines would be low, about ⅛", I knew this would result in a faux three-dimensional effect. The outlines would be nearly invisible with the body of the hooking gently slanting out into them to create a curved effect.

I planned this rug for my younger daughter's new mid-town condo, which has olive green–tinged hardwood floors throughout, so the background had to be green toned. This background gave me the most

pain to hook, but I worked through it in resignation and with persistence. Traditionally a Japanese family crest on a dark background is white, but because the rug was going on the floor, I thought white would be impractical. Instead, I spot-dyed the new warm, beige wool with tan, taupe, and khaki drab to get an "already soiled" effect. This "soiled" warm beige was also used as the background for the surrounding realistic oak leaves.

Fumiyo Heinig
Burlington, Ontario, Canada

Fumiyo has been rug hooking for about 15 years since her retirement. Before her daughters were born, she worked as a school psychologist in Toronto. When her daughters grew older, she taught the Japanese language at McMaster University and the University of Western Ontario.

In The Judges' Eyes

Unique design; well-balanced colors and motifs; effective use of high/low hooking. Color palette enhances the design; textures and hooking technique adds interest.

Daki-Gashiwa, 52" x 64", #6- and #8-cut hand-dyed and as-is wool on linen.
Designed and hooked by Fumiyo Heinig, Burlington, Ontario, Canada, 2015. CHRIS HAYHURST

Desert in Niger

capture these feelings is with structure, depths of color combinations, and the smoothness of the loops. I found the dome-like granaries and other buildings of clay bricks fascinating, and it gave me inspiration to keep drawing and redrawing, to keep adding shapes until it came together in a sketch I loved.

I transferred my design on linen and hooked with hand-dyed wool in #4 cuts and #5 cuts, using the monochromatic, analogous colors to show the depth of my feeling and space. I ended up with a design my mind could walk into and explore, both serene and sad. The mystery keeps talking to me as it hangs on my living room wall. It reminds me of life when treating the patients on the edge of the Sahara Desert. I used all my nursing skills possible for the patients we saw, and I left with a feeling that I have not done enough. I do not want Niger left unnoticed.

I started sewing at ten years of age, when my love affair with fabric began wanting to see colors moving with the change of light and weave. All types of needlework interested me, especially new uses of textiles. A friend taught me how to pull my first loops, with the gift of a hoop, a hook, and a Christmas wreath pattern. It was a wonderful start to the growing stages of learning fabric art.

I do my own designs now that have a story and a name by the time they are finished. Exploring each new rug or wall hanging teaches me more and pushes me to expand my techniques. Side by side, two wonderful wall hangings are on display by my adult daughter's paintings, showing our mutual love of art.

What a life I get to explore, and what a great art form to express it.

I have been on several international medical missions as a registered nurse. The three trips to Africa seem to persist in my thoughts, and I was looking for a way to speak of Galmi, Niger, Africa in the language of my fabric art. The beauty of the people in the desert, the isolation, and the desperation for health care with the sadness and sorrow talk to my heart. My way to

Kay Carmichael
Beaverton, Oregon

Kay has traveled internationally as a registered nurse. She first learned about rug hooking in 1999 after seeing hooked rugs in a friend's home. She's been hooking ever since.

Desert in Niger, 20" x 23", #4- and #5-cut hand-dyed wool on linen.
Designed and hooked by Kay Carmichael, Beaverton, Oregon, 2015. DALE LUTZ

Perfection; perfectly executed; beautiful technique; the colors and style of hooking contribute to the beauty of this abstract scene.

Fiddleheads

I grew up in Vermont where we foraged for fiddlehead ferns to eat in the early spring. My mother would sauté them in butter, and they were one of the first fresh "greens" of the year that were available to us after a long, cold winter. I was also inspired by a nautilus shell design I had punch hooked in 2015, and it reminded me of the spiral shape of the fiddlehead ferns as they emerge and unfurl.

I had always wanted to try hooking with velvet and thought that this fiddlehead piece would be a great place to start. I inherited a big bin of velvets from my mother and also used some hand-dyed pieces of velvet. I still wanted to create a wool rug, so I used the velvet to enhance and accent the design.

I love blue and use lots of blue in my hooking, so my goal was to avoid using any blue in this rug. I didn't succeed, but I tried not to use blue in the ferns, at least. My color plan was to use raspberry pink, yellow-green, and the various velvet colors I had, including red and purple. The background is one I've used before, dyed with layering blue, yellow, and red, providing a rich, subtly mottled backdrop to the ferns.

The piece came together pretty easily with the advice and guidance of my teacher at Cambria Pines Rug Camp, Diane Stoffel. There was mutual trust to try new things, and it was fun for both of us to watch it emerge from the backing. My favorite part of the piece is the overall spiraling effect found in the ferns and the background. The

spiral was what drew me to the design in the first place, and the background enhances the shape of the ferns.

My grandmother, Jane Olson, started me rug hooking in 1997. I had been familiar with the craft growing up, but I didn't try my hand at it until then. I enjoy hooking for so many reasons. I find it very relaxing, almost meditative, at the end of a long day. It helps me unwind and empties my mind so that I sleep better. I absolutely love the process of rug hooking, unlocking the puzzle of each pattern, solving its problems around color, design, and technique. It's the process that keeps me coming back for more. The finished product is ok, too!

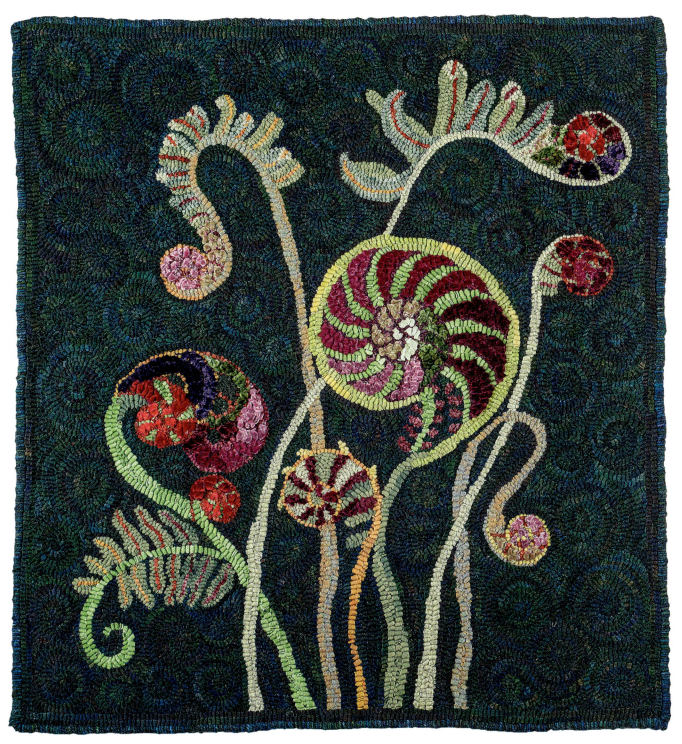

Fiddleheads, 24" x 26", #4- to 6-cut wool and hand-cut velvet on linen.
Designed and hooked by Brigitta Phy, Sebastopol, California, 2016. BRUCE SHIPPEE

Brigitta Bradford Phy
Sebastopol, California

Brigitta is a rug hooking teacher, designer, and supplier along with being a substitute teacher who's currently enrolled to become an elementary school teacher. She is the secretary of ATHA National and belongs to Wine Country Rug Hookers. This is her third appearance in Celebration.

Friendship

I hooked the spinning wheel first, followed by Jacqui and me, moving from the front of the rug to the back. I created this rug using a variety of materials, including Dorr wool, old clothes, and wool yarn that I had spun. I look at the threads like colors in a paint box that I can use to "paint" onto the canvas. Aside from some special accent colors, I tried choosing colors that closely matched reality.

The most challenging part for me was getting the spinning wheel just right. I don't have a spinning wheel of my own, so it was difficult to capture the shape properly. I referenced books and catalogues to get everything looking just right. While it was difficult to hook the faces since they're so small, my favorite part of the rug is the figure of Jacqui. I wanted to capture how gracious and kind she was, and I'm pleased with how it turned out.

I lived in Toronto, Canada, from 1976 to 1983, and I found a beautiful bell pull in the showcase of a library that my teacher, Fanie Sinclair, had made. I started learning with her in 1979, which is when I made my very first rug. It was so much fun getting the chance to learn a new art form since I had never even seen a hooked rug before.

It is a great honor for me to be chosen as a finalist. In Japan, the art of rug hooking isn't as well-known as it is in the United States or Canada. (Patchwork and quilting are, however, well-known.) I would like to spread the joy of this wonderful art for as long as possible.

I n 2014, I visited Milton, Australia, to attend a spinning workshop held by Miriam Miller. It was my first time spinning, and my friend and teacher Jacqui Thomson was kind and eager to teach me. It took me a few days to spin as my thread wasn't very smooth, but I caught on, little by little. It's a precious memory for me. I decided to paint this scene as the *suibokuga* (East Asian black ink painting) for the spring exhibition, and I used the sketch as the pattern to make this rug.

Fumiyo Hachisuka
Tokyo, Japan

Fumiyo is a rug hooker and sumi painter. She's been a member of TIGHR since 1994 and organizes the Rug Hooking Association in Tokyo. Friendship appeared in the 26th exhibition of the Rug Hooking Association in 2016. This is Fumiyo's fifth appearance in Celebration.

Background and leaves "embrace" subjects; great warmth in colors; interesting composition; subject matter and expressions tell the story of this friendship. Shading of leaves and hooking technique contribute to the overall excellence of this piece.

Friendship, 26" x 36", #3-cut Dorr's natural wool cloth, #5- and #6-cut as-is cloth, and hand-spun yarn on rug warp. Designed and hooked by Fumiyo Hachisuka, Tokyo, Japan, 2015.

Halifax Explosion

My grandmother, Lyda (Pettipas) Brewer, was a survivor of the Halifax Explosion in 1917. She was 11 years old at the time, watching the fire through the school window. When the window shattered from the shock wave, a piece of glass was embedded in her skull. She had that glass in her head until her death in her 90s. As a child, I could run my fingers over the lump when she told stories of the explosion. She was a truly inspirational woman, raising three children after she was widowed at a young age. This was a way to teach my grandchildren about her, since she passed away before they were born.

All of the photos of the Halifax Explosion are in black and white, but it was my hope to use the colors my grandmother would have seen looking out the window. I knew the ten-floor Acadia Sugar Refinery was made of brick and mortar, so the color choices there were simple. I did research on different elements, like the flags and ships, to ensure the colors matched what would have been found in 1917. My colors were dyed by my mother, Kaye Magwood, and a very good friend, Mr. Leslie Langille.

The Acadia Sugar Refinery was difficult to hook. There was no single picture showing the full view from the water. I also had to figure the actual scale of the building and replace parts of the original photos that were missing. There was no photo of the building from the same angle after the explosion, but I knew that it was leveled, then the snow that night buried what mounds of rubble existed.

The most meaningful section is the white ammunition ship, the Mont Blanc. Loaded with ammunition headed overseas, it was literally vaporized with very few pieces remaining. It has the most meaning to me because my great uncle had gone to work that morning, and after the explosion, he rushed home to find a hatch from the Mont Blanc had come through the roof and crushed his wife and 11-month-old son.

My rug was displayed at the memorial service for the Halifax Explosion in Halifax on December 6, 2016. It's making several appearances in 2017, including at the Yarmouth County Museum in Nova Scotia, at the Centreville Quilt and Rug Show, at the North End Library in Halifax, at the Lawrencetown Exhibition in Nova Scotia, and finally, in the Council Chambers of the Mayor of Boston as my thank you for the aid given to Halifax in the worst of times.

Halifax Explosion, 36½" x 24½", #2- to 4-cut hand-dyed and as-is wool on Scottish burlap. Designed and hooked by Leslie D. Magwood, Bridgetown, Nova Scotia, Canada, 2016.

Leslie Magwood
Bridgetown, Nova Scotia, Canada

Leslie started rug hooking 27 years ago after helping her mother, Kathleen Magwood, in her rug hooking classes. She has received national and international recognition for a rug she created for an editorial cartoonist on the shooting of Nathan Cirillo.

In The Judges' Eyes

Great emotion; amazing detail; captures the terrifying moment; spectacular!; stunning visualization of a disaster and its aftermath; the perspective and details are spot on.

Heathen Hill

This rug was based on a picture I took one wintery morning. I spent many winter weekends at a house just out of sight, past the mailbox. I love the mystery of Catskill winters. The picture of the winding road had been tucked away with other winter shots until a friend asked to see them. It had been several years since I last saw this picture, but I knew immediately it would be my next rug . . . tangled branches and all!

The picture I worked from is very monochromatic, so I knew the rug should be a gray-scale piece—basically, black, white, and gray in shades of brown. I have always worked with lots of colors in the past, so this was a pleasant challenge for me. For this piece, I used three tints of a warm brown, a dyed and natural Halcyon Geo gray, and white. There's a touch of red and blue in the mailbox and to my great joy, I saw a touch of yellow in the trees, so I had all of the primary colors! It was my favorite part of the piece because I got to express all the colors in the world in such a simple way.

I work in wool yarn, so yarn was a given. And the image screamed "yarn" with all of those twining branches. I was becoming dissatisfied with a bulky yarn's lack of structure, so I used this project to begin working with the Halcyon and Briggs and Little rug yarns. Halcyon Geo has a good textured gray yarn, which added depth to the piece, giving an illusion of many smaller branches, and Briggs and Little was the only rug-weight white yarn I could find. It was such a surprise to learn that natural yarn isn't white, and there was a 10–12-week back order for white yarn. I wound up finding some in stock in Canada that I was able to use.

With rug hooking, I feel that I have found my medium for expressing my thoughts about the world I see around me, especially landscapes. I work as a designer in the theatre, which is a communal art, but I have also always pursued my own individual expression through drawing, watercolor, and knitting. Hooking hit the spot. Hooking with yarn made my landscapes come alive in ways they had not before. It's a thrill.

Nancy Thun
Hoboken, New Jersey

Nancy is a theatre set and costume designer for Broadway shows, such as Mamma Mia *and* Jersey Boys. *She's a member of ATHA and Green Mountain Rug Hooking guild. This is her third appearance in* Celebration.

In The Judges' Eyes

Dynamic handling of snow on trees. Magnificent!; made me want to put on my boots and sweater; the title suggest foreboding, which the hooking and color convey.

Heathen Hill, 35" x 45", hand-dyed wool yarn on rug warp.
Designed and hooked by Nancy Thun, Hoboken, New Jersey, 2016.

Herring Cove

Herring Cove is a favorite spot in Provincetown, Massachusetts, to watch sunsets. The different textures and the sun's fading light are especially fascinating. The rug should draw you down the path to the water. It's this perspective that really draws you into the picture, and whenever I look at it, I'm brought back to Cape Cod at summer's end.

I wanted to use wool that I had on hand. The grays and browns worked well to depict the beach sand and represent the hills and valleys you'd find on a well-worn pathway. I adapted the picture I had to the wool, using colors that were realistic to the beach.

The most challenging part of the rug was hooking the fence. The way the light reflected on the slats was tricky to get just right and wound up taking me two or three attempts before I was satisfied. It taught me that it's important to keep working at a rug until you're happy with the result, even if you need to re-do parts of it. To finish the rug, I used cotton cording, rug yarn, and cotton binding tape. I was proud that this rug won Best of Division in Traditional Rug Hooking at the Eastern States Exposition 2016.

I first started rug hooking when I went to sign up for a rug braiding class in 2009 and was intrigued by the rug hooking that was on display. I've loved rug hooking (and rug braiding) ever since. I'm a thwarted art major who spent thirty years making computer infrastructure maps before retiring and discovering the wonderfully satisfying world of rug hooking. It's enjoyable because the subject matter is whatever you want it to be. It's relaxing, challenging, fun, and the final piece is something you can actually use.

Robin Salmaggi
Florence, Massachusetts

Robin is a retired GIS professional. She belongs to the Quabbin chapter (Region 1) of ATHA and has won prizes at the Eastern States Exposition from 2013–2016.

In The Judges' Eyes

Masterful use of directional hooking; subtle color plan enhances serenity of scene; excellent details.

Herring Cove, 38" x 27", #4- to 6-cut hand-dyed, reclaimed, and as-is wool on linen. Designed and hooked by Robin Salmaggi, Florence, Massachusetts, 2016.

Just a Cat

I was first inspired to make this rug after taking a workshop with Capri Boyle Jones, who emphasized a painter style. When I researched Capri's work, I was super excited to learn from her. Her work inspired me to go through my photographs, and I selected two pictures that I had taken on our family farm: one of the cat and one that was a close-up of flowers. Capri suggested combining the two photos for the rug and drew the design onto the linen. The cat was my favorite part. It was one of many barn cats that explored around the farm. It didn't have a name and wasn't a pet, thus the title, *Just a Cat*.

I wanted to use colors that closely matched the farm cillat and garden. Capri helped me select wools that would depict foreground, middle ground, and background and taught the importance of using a variety of bright and dull wools along with light and dark wools. I learned how important it was to have lots of values for each color in the piece.

The trickiest part for me was getting the eyes just right. I had my rug completed and bound but didn't feel like the cat's eyes conveyed exactly what I wanted. A conversation with Donna Hrkman helped me change the eyes from "OK" to "Yes!" I finished the rug by using the "fold forward" method and bound it with wool yarn.

I love all fiber arts. I weave on my loom, I always have a quilt in the works, and I'm currently trying my hand at thread painting. I was first introduced to rug hooking, however, after a kind friend invited me to attend a meeting "just to see what the group is like." The group was welcoming, and I immediately wanted to try my hand. I enjoy rug hooking for so many reasons. The rugs themselves add a decorative touch to any room and look great whether they're hanging on the walls or lying on the floor. Well-dyed wool is so beautiful and luscious. And the other rug hookers I've met have been a wonderful group of people.

Starr Atwell
Columbus, Indiana

Starr is a retired elementary and middle school art teacher. She belongs to ATHA, Puckihuddlers, and a small local rug group. This is her second appearance in Celebration.

In The Judges' Eyes

Penetrating, thoughtful eyes; terrific!; well-designed composition that is full of intriguing details; love the artistic expression of the flowers.

Just a Cat, 24¾" x 30", #5- and #7-cut wool on linen.
Designed by Starr Atwell and Capri Boyle Jones and hooked by Starr Atwell, Columbus, Indiana, 2015. JOHN RHOADES

Liberty

During our visits to Colonial Williamsburg, we had interacted with many of the amazing historic interpreters, and I noticed the words "Liberty or death" embroidered on some of their summer linen jackets. While it was a phrase that everyone had heard, I wanted to know more. Spoken eloquently by Patrick Henry on March 23, 1775, at the Second Virginia Convention in Richmond, the words, "I know not what course others may take; but as for me, give me liberty or give me death!" punctuated Henry's now famous speech. He was a delegate to that Convention, and he had proposed, over the objections of many others, raising a militia to protect the colony of Virginia in the desperate days before the American Revolution.

The colors I used are a worn version of the traditional red, white, and blue. The red in this flag is really a rust color with highlights of gold. The wool was dyed by Marian Hall of Wooly Dye Works in Pennsylvania. Marian used the abrash method of dyeing to enhance a really mottled effect in the wool. It was chosen to give life to an eighteenth-century version of a hand-woven red. It offers depth and just the right amount of inconsistency needed to create a sense of time-worn beauty.

My favorite part was hooking the words. Type is essential to the projects I work on in my day job as a graphic designer, so it feels really natural to incorporate words into my rug designs. The word "Liberty" was a hand-drawn compilation of several different typefaces created by modern designers. The words "or death" were drawn based solely on Caslon Antique, a typeface created from type inspired by an eighteenth-century London engraver, William Caslon I, who worked in the tradition of what is now called old-style serif letter design. I hooked these words in very subtle variations of dark blue with tiny highlights of light wool in a method I usually reserve for hooking an object.

Creating the folds in the fabric was the challenging aspect of this rug. It required the use of light and color to make the folds appear natural and almost three-dimensional. It was where I learned about the difficulties of hooking a design that depends on perspective and light.

I love rug hooking because it's a very expressive art. I started rug hooking in 1999 after picking up a library book on a whim. While you are limited by materials in some senses—a backing material, fiber, and a hook—there is no limit on imagination. It's accessible but complex, a perfect combination for an artist.

Ellen Banker
Williamsburg, Virginia

Ellen is a graphic designer. She belongs to ATHA, the Green Mountain Rug Hooking Guild, and the Goose Creek Rug Hookers. She is a contributing writer for Rug Hooking *magazine, and her book on introducing words into a hooked rug will be released in 2018.*

In The Judges' Eyes

Superb rendering of iconic symbol; exceptional lettering; wonderful folds.

Liberty, 48" x 34". #3-, #4- and #6-cut dyed wool on linen.
Designed and hooked by Ellen Banker, Williamsburg, Virginia, 2016. LYNN BOHANNON

My Son, Jesse

While visiting my son, Jesse, and his wife in Vancouver, we stopped at a brew pub. I took a photo of Jesse, and when I looked at it, I couldn't resist the challenge of hooking him. I had previously hooked a portrait of my daughter, Christy, and felt the need to "even things up."

I loved the cheeky look in Jesse's eyes the most. My instructor, Donna Hrkman, suggested I hook the eyes first, and it was heartwarming to see them following me throughout the hooking process. The background wood ended up being the most challenging part. I hooked it last and was eager to be finished. I kept remembering my mother saying "haste makes waste," so I had to slow myself down.

I did some casserole/spot dyeing for the background wood and hair. When I looked at the photo, I found it interesting to find colors I didn't initially expect like bits of green in his hair and using several values of blue in his shirt. I love dyeing wool. It is exciting to pull a pot of dyeing off the stove or out of the oven to see the resulting magic. When the wool comes out of the dryer, the first thing I feel like doing is wrapping myself in it, putting it to my face, and inhaling its scent.

I usually hook very colorful and vibrant pieces. Once in a while, I challenge myself and move out of my comfort zone. By overcoming the challenges of hooking a fine-shaded and realistic piece like this, I realized that I was capable of anything if I put my mind to it. It was gratifying to see the look of joy in my son's face when I presented the hooking to him. I feel like I have left him a beautiful legacy.

After watching my mother-in-law hook for years, I finally picked up a hook in 1988, and I haven't stopped since. Throughout my childhood, I was surrounded by textiles as my mother was a beautiful seamstress and quilter. I enjoy rug hooking because I love the feel of the wool and the repetitive action of pulling up loops, not to mention the process of designing, working through challenges, and, not surprisingly, the excitement that comes with finishing a project. I'm a certified McGown instructor, and I love teaching as well. I find students and my hooking friends inspiring, and I get a lot of satisfaction seeing their completed works.

In The Judges' Eyes

His facial expression is a work of art! Hooked frame is excellent; background and shirt hooked in an interesting and delightful manner.

My Son, Jesse, 13½" x 13½", #3- to 5-cut hand-dyed wool on linen.
Designed and hooked by Cec Caswell, Sherwood Park, Alberta, Canada, 2016.

Cec Caswell
Sherwood Park, Alberta, Canada

Cec is a textile artist who teaches coast to coast in Canada. One of her rugs has been purchased by the Royal Alberta Museum, and she was voted Readers' Choice for original designs in All-Time Favorite Hand-Hooked Rugs. This is her fifth appearance in Celebration.

My Two Loves

My *Two Loves* shows my children exploring the world, sometimes together and sometimes by themselves. I wanted to show how they're beginning to let go of my hand more often now than they used to and that although they are still so young, they are already their own little people. I chose my images to capture their curiosity and their dawning ambitions as well as my own pride in them and my own hope for the strength of their sibling love to carry them through the future together. The idea for the project came after my daughter walked out alone onto a red sandstone outcrop overlooking the sea in Îles-de-la-Madeleine, Quebec, to watch the waves. I was nervous, and I wouldn't have walked the same path myself. I had sharp thoughts for my husband for showing it to her, but then I took her picture because she was so completely at ease. I was proud of her, and I began watching them both differently afterwards.

As their mother, I cannot help but love the two images in the middle column the most. I'm sure that moments of undisguised sibling love such as these melt the hearts of mothers everywhere. It also doesn't hurt that I felt the most confident with the technical aspects of the hand-in-hand image, and so the hooking was enjoyable and stress free.

The most challenging aspect of this piece was making the faces. These are my first attempts at faces. I knew that that even a single misplaced loop would be obvious and off-putting. I worked up to this challenge by beginning with the images containing side profiles, detailed hair, and full-length figures. Once I was comfortable with that, I moved to the front of the face, and finally to the three-quarter profiles. On the one hand, several of my errors emphatically confirmed my initial trepidation that even a single loop can ruin a face. However, patience, careful observation, the practice developed from my staged approach, and the fine resolution achievable with yarn made the challenge more pleasant than I had anticipated.

This project embodies all of the freedom that I love about rug hooking. When I teach, I try to impart to my students that they are free to see what they love in the world and capture it in their own art. The only technique that matters is what lets you capture what is in your imagination.

My Two Loves, 57½" x 49", wool yarn, acrylic yarn, and metallic yarn on linen. Designed and hooked by Karen Miller, Ottawa, Ontario, Canada, 2016.
DANIEL MACDONALD

Karen Miller
Ottawa, Ontario, Canada

Karen is an artist who works out of her studio in Ottawa, Canada. Her work has won several awards, including a 2015 ARTicipate Grant and a 2012 Viewer's Choice Award at Hooking in the Mountains XVI. This is her fourth appearance in Celebration.

In The Judges' Eyes

Love this! Creative format and skillfully hooked; realistic hair and red coat exceptionally well done. I feel the love; wonderful memories.

Northwest Passage

I live in the beautiful Pacific Northwest. One of the annual traditions of nature is the passage of the Chinook salmon and the meeting of wildlife at the river. Bears and their young gather to eat their fill before the harsh winter ahead. In celebration of this event, I wanted to create a rug that displays the vibrancy and splendor of this yearly cycle.

I wanted this rug to celebrate the amazing colors of autumn. I started this rug by drawing two salmon and filling them in with the rusty reds and greens of the spawning Chinook. I wanted the river and salmon to "pop" with color as the main focus of the rug while the bear, frog, turtle, and dragonfly

blend more into the gorgeous backdrop of trees, scrub brush, and the river's edge. Nature blends animals into their surroundings for their safety (even the brown bear), and I wanted my rug to convey this.

About ten years ago, I sustained a brain injury in a car accident. After brain surgery, I suddenly found colors to be brighter and I could actually draw. As therapy for my hand tremor, I taught myself to hook rugs. As a result of my brain injury, I have a more unconventional approach to rug hooking. I do not draw out entire designs or plan my colors in advance. In fact, I didn't decide on including the bear until I was more than halfway finished with the rug. I like to draw

a section of the design, then turn the rug upside down and fill in the remainder of the rug with color. I find that by turning the rug upside down that I don't focus too much on the design or lines but rather on the colors and shadowing instead.

Since my injury, I can't tolerate a lot of noise or activity. Rug hooking has been an amazing outlet for me. This is my 42nd rug in ten years. I have discovered a creativity that I didn't know I had before the accident. My favorite part is going into my wool room with all of the gorgeous colors and choosing what to work with next.

Northwest Passage, 40" x 41", #4- to 6-cut hand-dyed and as-is wool and yarn for edging on monk's cloth.
Designed and hooked by Sharon Stapleton, Salem, Oregon, 2016. JAMES SOUTHWORTH

Sharon Stapleton
Salem, Oregon

Sharon is a retired pediatric critical care nurse and flight nurse. She has won numerous first and second place awards over the past ten years at the Oregon State Fair. This is her second appearance in Celebration.

Powerful interpretation; motifs speak of forward movement and power; I love the folk art quality of the motifs. The design complements the theme dramatically; lovely color palette.

Peggy's Cove

Usually I hook rugs of places that are important to my family's history. This rug is different. It's a stranger's house in Peggy's Cove, Nova Scotia. I was inspired by it because it's how I would have drawn a house when I was a child—a square with a pointed roof and a door in the middle with a window on either side, a window upstairs, and of course a chimney just barely off to one side. The function of the house dictated the design. There's no ornamentation, no fakery, and no pretense of being anything but what it is.

I have hooked these clapboard houses of the Maritimes before, so I had what I needed on hand. This is a more subdued palette than I usually choose. The little house was painted white over cedar shingles against the overcast blue-gray sky. For the clapboard cottage, I used white Dorr wool and pleated it when wet, held it in place with straight pins, and then placed it in a small puddle of Cushing's Silver Gray dye. This Shibori technique gave me horizontal stripes of gray and white.

The vegetation was my favorite part to hook. There were all of these greens mixed with golds that looked really beautiful. I was able to put tweeds to good use here by using some in the vegetation and then using some black-and-white tweeds for the granite rocks.

The overhead wires were the most challenging aspect. I wanted them to look like they were sloping down gently, but the grid of the linen made them appear jagged like stairs. To combat that, I used woolen yarn and cut most of the loops to make a finer line that sloped the way I wanted it to. It was a conscious decision to include the wires. I've spent years taking photographs and crouching down to avoid wires. But they're part of the skyline too and ought to be included.

I have hooked quite a few houses that are significant to my own family's history. This house must have a story too, but it's one that I don't know. There aren't any visible clues to suggest anything about the family that lives there now—no bicycles or baby carriages out front or lobster traps or fishing gear along the sides of the house. The human narrative is a mystery, and in this way, it's different from the houses I have hooked in the past.

Peggy's Cove, 13½" x 13¾", #2-, #3-, #4-, & #6-cut wool on linen.
Designed and hooked by Trish Johnson, Toronto, Ontario, Canada, 2016.

Trish Johnson
Toronto, Ontario, Canada

Trish is involved in many artistic pursuits, including photography and quilting. She's a member of the Upper Toronto Guild and the Georgetown Guild. This is her eleventh rug in Celebration and she has won three Reader's Choice awards.

In The Judges' Eyes

Subtle variations create calmness; nicely hooked house and foliage; makes me want to know more.

Red Glasses

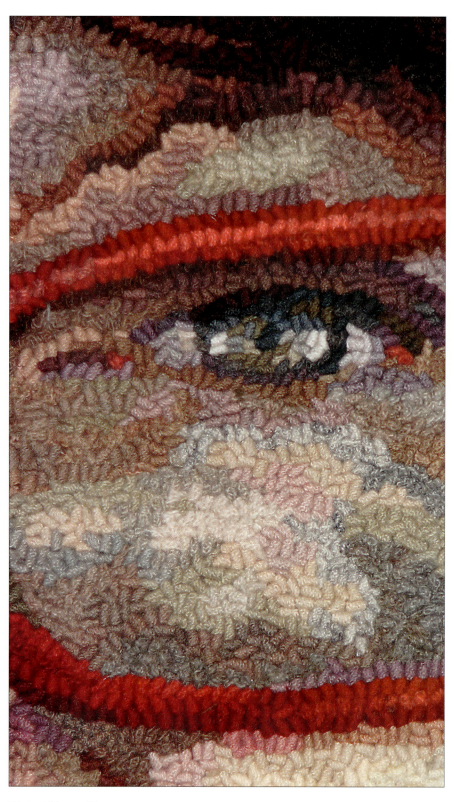

My intent with this piece was to experiment with a wool palette in muted grays, browns, and reds to be used in portraiture hooking. To do this, I dyed 8-value swatches of 13 colors in both plain and textured wool. The most challenging part of this rug was getting the color just right. I started out with too many muted colors and the skin looked dead. So I kept reverse hooking and adding bright and more intense colors until I was able to wake up the skin so that it looked lively. I learned that gray works best in small quantities and that rugs must have intense and bright colors alongside muted colors for the rug to come alive.

The hooking technique I use is called zonalism. Zonalism focuses on hooking different value zones of the photograph instead of reproducing exact colors or trying to shade as traditional rug hookers do. I developed this technique to create impressionistic hooked mats using family photographs as visuals for my pattern. The other difference is my hooked stitch. I never hook straight rows, which leaves lines and sharp contrast when a new color is added. Rather I use a pebble stitch in order to control the blending of values of different colors in the same zone. The pebble stitch is created using a random-walk pattern. When one loop is pulled up, the next loop has to touch the previous loop but cannot be pulled up in a straight ditch or row. In zonalism, there are no hooked rows, but rather hooked areas with random edges where new color is seeded into the crevices.

I was inspired to create this rug because I had just bought a new pair of fun red glasses and wanted to capture them in a self-portrait. Hooking the glasses themselves was my favorite part of the rug since it brought me so much joy to wear them. I wound up hooking them twice to get the color just right, and I'm pleased with how they turned out.

I began rug hooking in 1995 in rural Michigan. I took a beginning rug hooking class at Waterloo Historical Farm and began exhibiting my rugs at historical festivals in Michigan and Illinois. I love to rug hook because it's my creative and meditative outlet that helps me keep a balanced life.

Red Glasses, 30" x 30", #6-cut hand-dyed wool on linen.
Designed and hooked by April D. DeConick, Houston, Texas, 2016.

April DeConick
Houston, Texas

April is an award-winning hooked wool artist and master dyer. She is the author of two rug hooking books: The Wool Palette and Wool Snapshots. She has written articles for the ATHA Newsletter and Rug Hooking magazine. This is her sixth appearance in Celebration.

In The Judges' Eyes

Realistic portrait using blocks of color; great use of values for lights and shadows; wonderful eyes and smile that make for a great self-portrait.

Reflecting....

T amara Pavich, a wonderfully talented writer for *Rug Hooking* magazine, asked me if I would like to contribute a rug to her new book about self-exploration in rug hooking. Here I'm attempting to portray myself exploring my second passion (next to rug hooking, of course), which is genealogy. Since I am very interested in ancestry and love photos, I decided I would try to attach one of my favorite photos (of myself feeding my three lambs) to a rug.

I used traditional 100% new Dorr wool for this rug, along with repurposed wool. I also purchased fabric from Red Barn Rugs. The smoothness and high quality of the Dorr wool enhanced the flesh and smooth blue shirt fabric as well as the white book

pages, and the texture of the striped fabric behind the mirror makes the wall look real. The photo(s) of myself in the rug are actually just that—photos on fabric. I couldn't hook them small enough to be clearly seen, so I took them to a professional printer and had him print the photos on a white piece of fabric. I added polyester batting to the back of the photos, so they would be the same height as the wool loops. Then I simply hand sewed the two photos to the rug warp backing and hooked the rest of the rug around them. It worked like a charm.

I love sepia colors and started out using only those colors, but when I added my blue shirt, red glasses, and pink flowers, I saw how the colors enhanced the rug. For the striped

color on the wall behind the mirror, I asked a color expert, my friend Cathy Stephen from Red Barn Rugs, to help me. She knew exactly what wool to choose, and I'm so happy with it.

I first became interested in rug hooking after I took a beginner's class in 1996. After completing three or four small pieces, I put everything away for 17 years, and after retiring, I picked it up and started loving it all over again in 2013. Rug hooking is very stress reducing for me. I'm at home and caring for my husband who has Alzheimer's, so it's nice to be near him while enjoying my rug hooking, too. Besides, I love a challenge and have always loved anything fiber related.

Marilyn Becker
Wausau, Wisconsin

Marilyn is a happily retired rug hooker. She belongs to TIGHR, The Australian Rug Makers Guild, ATHA (Wisconsin Rug Hooking Guild, Chapter 7), and her local group, Wool Inspirations. This is her fourth appearance in Celebration.

In The Judges' Eyes

Captures the mood; nice rendition of old photo; clever design that is well realized; leaves provide nice infusion of color.

Reflecting...., 30½" x 42", #3- to 7-cut hand-dyed and repurposed wool on cotton rug warp.
Designed and hooked by Marilyn Becker, Wausau, Wisconsin, 2016.

River Rug

My husband and I have traveled extensively. Without really planning to, we have cruised on many of the major rivers of the world. Sally Ballinger suggested that I design and hook a story rug of our river travels, so that's what I did.

The five rivers I decided to feature (starting at the top) include the Amazon River where pink dolphins and toucans live. The brown around the dolphin is where the Rio Negro meets the Amazon. Then there's the Seine River in Paris, featuring the Eiffel Tower and the Toulouse Lautrec Cancan girls. It was the most challenging section for me because I wanted the feeling of fireworks, but I had to find a way to make both the dark Eiffel Tower and the very light Cancan dancers stand out. I did a lot of careful selection with the spot-dyed wool. The Rhine River in Germany near the Marksburg Castle is next. The hills are solid vineyards, and every town has its own wines! Next is the Yangtze River in China, featuring the Seven Gorges and the fishermen who use cormorants to dive for fish. I also include the Xian terra cotta warriors and the blue and white porcelain pottery. Finally, there's the Nile River in Egypt. We rode camels out into the desert, saw the pyramids, and rode on a native felucca boat.

I used many different dye techniques to create this rug, including swatch dyeing for fine shading, spot dyeing for special effects, and batch dyeing for the border design. I chose colors that would realistically depict all the places we traveled.

I learned to hook with different cuts of wool with this rug. Up to this point, I had only used #8 cut. Sally Ballinger taught me fine shading with #3. I also learned several methods of dyeing wool. I feel like I broke into a whole new level of rug hooking!

I first got started in 2006 when I bought a frame, hook, and project from a friend who decided she didn't like rug hooking. After exchanging the hook for one that was better, I discovered how much fun rug hooking was and how having the right tool can really make a big difference. I love rug hooking because it's a multi-faceted art form, offering me endless challenges and learning experiences. I have hooked 40 rugs in the last 10 years, and I can't wait to create more.

Jane Witmer
Big Pine Key, Florida

Jane was a production potter for 45 years, making blue and white decorative functional ware. She's a member of the National Guild of Pearl K. McGown. This is her first appearance in Celebration.

In The Judges' Eyes

Good composition that enhances the details; delightful story rug; well-conceived and executed.

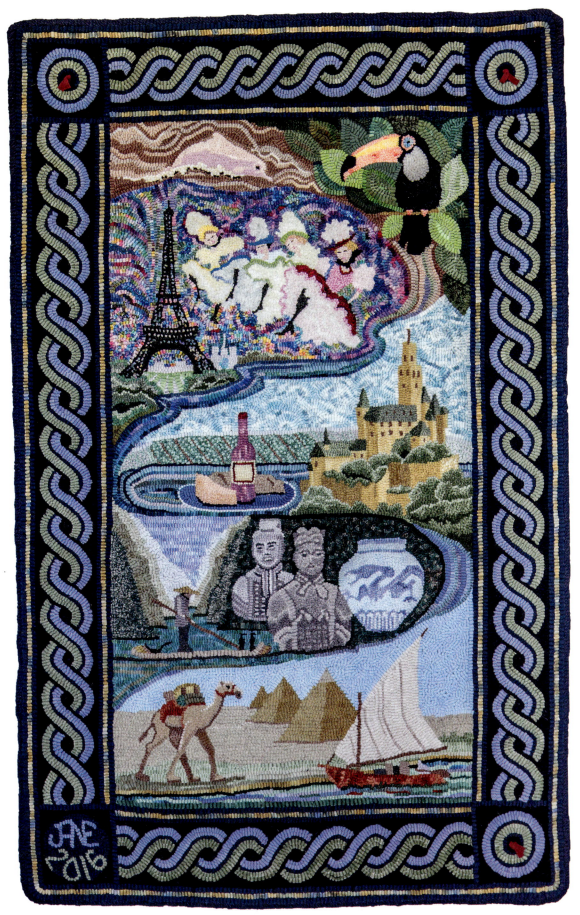

River Rug, 28" x 43", #3-, #5-, #7- and #8-cut wool on linen.
Designed and hooked by Jane Witmer, Big Pine Key, Florida, 2016. SYLVIE STOLL

The Circus Rolls into Town

On a trip to the Circus World Museum in Baraboo, Wisconsin, I became fascinated with the colors and design of the antique circus wagon wheels. There were so many variations both in color and style. I am drawn to geometric forms, and these certainly caught in eye. After taking numerous photos of the wheels, I decided they would make a good rug.

I chose to do this piece in #2, #3, and #4 cuts of wool, so I could capture the detail of the wheel designs. I did not embellish this piece with other fibers because I felt like the wheels had enough personality. The colors of the wheels are as they appeared on the wagons. I tried to pick background colors that would make the wheels stand out, and some dip-dyed wool

was used to imitate the flame painting on the wheels.

The border was very challenging to design and hook. I took four different wheels, cut the rim of each, and then laid it flat to get the pattern for each of the four borders. It was difficult to get the patterns to fit evenly in the space and even harder to hook them finely enough not to lose any detail. I used two colors of rug binding—a dark color for the borders and a lighter color for the corners—to avoid distracting from the piece itself.

I first got started in rug hooking after reading an article in the May 1971 issue of *Woman's Day* magazine, featuring hooked rugs. I thought, "Wow, those would look great in home with our antiques. I think I'll

try making one." I completed my first rug, a Texas star pattern, in 1972, and it's still being used in our front hall today. I hooked several more rugs and then took 15 years off to do weaving and other handwork. I started again in 1989 when I attended my first Cream City Rug Hookers Guild meeting, and I haven't stopped since.

I love rug hooking for so many reasons: the camaraderie, the creativity, the enjoyment of designing and color planning, and the meditative quality of just pulling up the loops. I've been involved with many textile techniques, including weaving, knitting, silk screening, cross stitch, felting, and prodding. I keep coming back to rug hooking as my favorite media. It really lets me express my creativity.

The Circus Rolls into Town, 38" x 38", #2- to 5-cut hand-dyed and as-is wool on linen.
Designed and hooked by Lyle Drier, Waukesha, Wisconsin, 2016. DENNIS DRIER

Lyle Drier
Waukesha, Wisconsin

Lyle recently retired from the antiques business after 41 years. The Circus Rolls into Town *won first place and Best of Show at the Wisconsin State Fair in 2016. This is her eleventh appearance in* Celebration, *including a past appearance on the cover.*

The Gathering

I was inspired to make this rug because I had never tried making animals before. I'm a fairly new rug hooker, so I wanted to expand my knowledge and skill by trying new things that I haven't done before. I was interested in the proddy style and wanted to incorporate that into this work. The manes were perfect for that. This piece taught me when and how to use the proddy technique and how important it is to have a real eye for animals.

Although the water in Africa would probably not be the beautiful blue-gray I used, I liked how it created a nice contrast against their neutral bodies. The zebra's ears were my favorite part of this piece. I was able to incorporate some of my own dog's white hair to create ear tufts, giving it a more natural feel to the inside of an animal's ear.

I finished the rug by wrapping it onto a thin board and stapled it. I wanted to piece to be taut so the muscle structures of the face and necks would be more visible.

I first became interested in rug hooking after seeing a local artist featured in a local newspaper. I love to do it because it's a simple technique that can yield varied results. There are so many versatile elements from the materials to the colors to the sizes of the cuts. Plus it's portable, so I can work on my piece anywhere, whenever the mood strikes me.

I enjoy all sorts of fiber activities. I make tuffets, mystical armature sculptures, window treatments, upholstery, and more. I began rug hooking six years ago, and I love it. I often have a hard time leaving it and work on each of my pieces intensely. I keep a folder of next projects, which just gets bigger and bigger. I have started to go to guild shows near my home and always get inspired by the pieces others are producing. There is no end to the possibilities that exist for this art form, and I can't wait to work on my next project.

Kerri Kolbe
Bolton, Connecticut

Kerri used to work as a director in a finance institution in technology, heading a data mining and analytics department. She is now happily retired. She is a member of the Green Mountain Guild.

In The Judges' Eyes

You feel you could touch them; fascinating subject matter; captures the moment; looks like a photo; amazing color contrast; love the water movement.

The Gathering, 32" x 50½", #4-cut hand-dyed wool on linen.
Designed and hooked by Kerri Kolbe, Bolton, Connecticut, 2015.

Transformation

I have a habit of stalking butterflies to get photos of them and was delighted when I captured a photo of the Eastern tiger swallowtail butterfly enjoying Joe Pye weed. Originally, I thought I would do a painting, but once I learned how to rug hook, I knew this photo would be perfect for that medium. While my original photo is beautiful, this hooked piece brings the butterfly back to life.

This piece was my first time hooking with fibers other than wool. Since butterflies have a shimmery effect, I wanted to use fabrics that also reflected the light in interesting ways. The velvet, sari silk, satin, and ribbon added great depth and interest to the butterfly. Black yarn gave the body of the butterfly a fuzzy look. At first, I intended

to hook the Joe Pye weed with wool, but I decided to try making them look three dimensional. I searched the craft stores for yarn and eventually found an acrylic yarn that was the correct color. After hooking the flowers high, I clipped only some of their loops to make it more realistic.

I learned a lot about the anatomy of the butterfly. At first, I thought the lines in the wings were random, but after a closer look, I realized they had clear paths to certain areas on the edges. This whole process gave me a new appreciation for a creature I had already greatly admired.

I hooked the butterfly first, and when it came to hook the rest of the piece, the background, I was unsure how to proceed. There's a photography term called "bokeh,"

which refers to the out-of-focus blur in the background of a photo. I tried analyzing the photograph but decided I needed another way to look at it. On my computer, I simplified the photo with an editing program to make it look more like a poster to help define patches of color that were otherwise more difficult to see. It was that effect that I recreated in my rug.

This piece signifies not only the transformation that a caterpillar goes through to become a butterfly or what a photo goes through to become a hooked art piece, it also signifies a time when I went from being a homeschooling mom to an "on the road" artist. Life is full of transformations, often painful and difficult, but still beautiful in the end.

Transformation, 19" x 19", #4- to 8-cut dyed and as-is wool, velvet, satin, sari silk, yarn, and ribbon on linen. Designed and hooked by Janine Broscious, Monrovia, Maryland, 2016.

Janine Broscious
Monrovia, Maryland

Janine is an RV-ing artist grandma who designs patterns and sells them on her website along with handmade jewelry. She also writes articles for Rug Hooking magazine. This is her first appearance in Celebration.

In The Judges' Eyes

Nice composition; lovely colors; luscious color and good use of alternate materials.

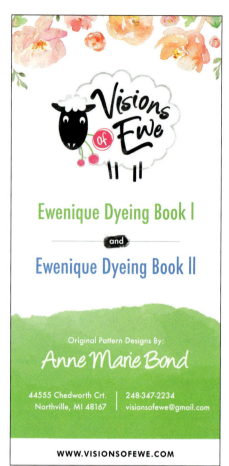

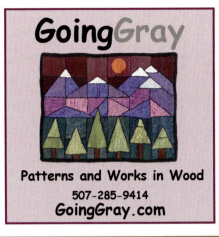

California Strawberry Thief

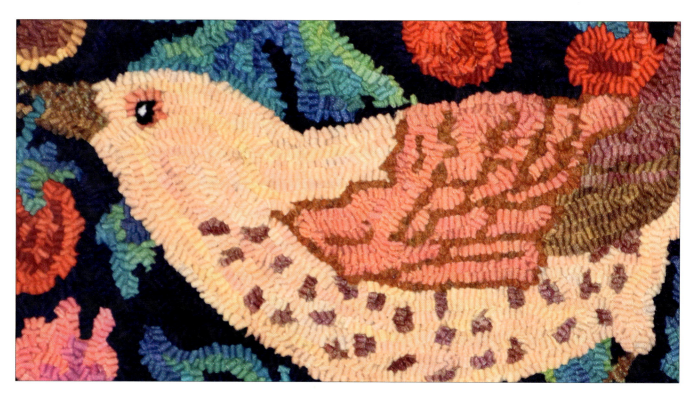

I love the works of William Morris, and when I saw this design, I knew I had to hook it. I'm a student of Gene Shepherd's and love using his hand-dyed wools, particularly the dump dyes. Dump dyes allowed me to have lively colors that coordinated together nicely. I limited the use of different textures so that the piece would have a smooth, pure look.

This was my first bird, and I worked with Diane Stoffel to get it just right. Diane is a fantastic teacher and was able to effectively communicate how to tackle this complex subject. I worked with Gene Shepherd to color plan the rug. I wanted the rug to be lively, not somber, and made use of the dump dyes. For the background, I settled on eggplant and bled some of the color out of it. It was still dark like I wanted, but it harmonized well with all of the colors and set them off in a much softer way than a pure black would have.

The pattern for this rug was complex, and when it was on my frame, a 14" orbiter, it was difficult to see clearly what I was working on. To tackle this, I developed a color scheme and colored in sections of the pattern to represent different objects, such as leaves, branches, flowers, etc., to help me keep everything in perspective. I finished the rug by crocheting a shell pattern along the border. The yarn I used was a hand-dyed brown, which created a stylized edge to the piece.

I can thank my dogs for getting me into rug hooking. Right before I retired, I had all of the carpet removed from my home and had tile installed. This was much better for my dogs, but I thought I still needed to have rugs on the floors. So in 2013, now retired, I looked up how to make traditional rugs on the Internet and found Gene Shepherd's YouTube page. I bought a kit and haven't stopped hooking since. I was delighted to learn that I live relatively close to Gene, so I'm able to join in on his hook-ins. I love rug hooking because I love working with color, truly "painting" with the wool. I also appreciate the rug hooking community and have developed very special friendships from the gatherings I've attended.

Gretchen Bolar
Corona, California

Gretchen is the retired Vice Chancellor at the University of California. She is a member of the Orange Coast Classics chapter of ATHA. This is her first appearance in Celebration.

The scalloped edge nicely reflects the dip-dyed border design elements; crochet edging mirroring the design adds that little extra.

California Strawberry Thief, 50½" x 32", #4-, #5-, #6-, #7-, and #9-cut wool with hand-dyed wool yarn for whipping on primitive linen. Designed by Encompassing Designs (William Morris) and hooked by Gretchen Bolar, Corona, California, 2016. GENE SHEPHERD

Cattails and Dragonflies

After looking at abundant photos of dragonflies online, I selected five favorites to use for my color inspiration. In addition to hand-dyed wool fabric, I used yarns, velvet, silk sari ribbon, nylon stockings, knitted yard goods, metallic threads, and sheer polyester fabric cut into 1-to 1 ½-inch strips. It surprised me that the pink wings of the upper right-hand dragonfly used up about three-quarters of a yard of sheer polyester fabric! In some of the dragonflies, I incorporated sculpted hooking, using either a #3 cut or a #4 cut. Two of the strap leaves also have sculpting. The sky background has five different hand-dyed wools.

While some people may enjoy dyeing wool as much or more than the actual hooking, I am not one of those people. I dye when I need something specific that I can't find in my wool stash or easily purchase. I'm much more interested in crafting the rug itself.

I finished the rug with triple cording because I thought it would make the rug look like it was framed and give it extra stiffness to help it hang well without waffling. I came away from this project with a new appreciation for alternative fibers. They can do as much to enhance a rug as choosing the right texture of wool.

I first became interested in rug hooking after seeing a small hooked piece in a quilt shop. I didn't even know what to call it at the time, but it was like nothing I'd ever seen before. The quilt shop was offering a class, and the rest is history. Rug hooking fulfills my hunger for creativity. There is always more to learn and so many fabulous teachers to help. It's very rewarding to create a thing of beauty that also has a utilitarian purpose.

I was asked to develop this pattern as a show-and-tell assignment for the North Central McGown Teachers Workshop. I didn't hesitate because it was a beautifully designed pattern with the potential to incorporate all sorts of alternative fibers.

As soon as I saw this pattern, I knew I would be doing considerable hoving or sculpting, also known as hooking in Waldoboro style named after the city of Waldoboro, Maine, where that style of hooking was developed. I couldn't wait to get at the cattails and the segmented bodies of some of the dragonflies to do a bit of sculpting. The 3-D hooking added to the realism of the design.

Terryl A. Ostmo
Wahpeton, North Dakota

Terryl is a fiber artist who's been rug hooking since 1998. She's a member of ATHA, the National McGown Guild, Greater Midwest Teachers Workshop, and North Central McGown Teachers Workshop. This is her third appearance in Celebration.

In The Judges' Eyes

Love the use of alternative materials and sculpturing; exciting colors with excellent use of sculpting; ephemeral; masterful use of fibers.

Cattails and Dragonflies, 24" x 42", hand-dyed wool, wool yarn, polyester sheer fabric, nylon stockings, metallic threads, velvet yardage, and silk sari ribbon on rug warp. Designed by Norma Batistini and hooked by Terryl Ostmo, Wahpeton, North Dakota, 2016.

Cheltenham

My sister, Shirley, asked me if I would hook a large rug for her dining room. It's hard to find a design for a very large rug, but Martina's pattern repeated nicely. The open design of the corners of the pattern created a secondary motif when repeated that worked well with the central motif. Plus, the geometric nature of the design complemented the many quilted pieces my sister has in her home. My sister loved the rug so much that instead of putting it in her dining room, she made it the centerpiece in her living room!

Because my sister's house is sunny, I chose to use mostly off-the-bolt textured wool to reduce fading. I did dye a spot dye that I used in various places—the veins of the leaves, the center of some of the pom-pom flowers, in between the layers of the halo around the major motif, and in the flowers in the secondary motif. I hoped this wool would help unify the various elements of the rug. I also dyed the yellow for the tips of the green leaves and used a 6-value swatch for the halo.

The only request my sister had was that I incorporate burgundy and hunter green since these were the accent colors in her living room and dining room. She also loves the color purple, so I decided to hook the rug with fall colors: green, burgundy, yellow, orange, purple, and brown. Working with the orange plaid was the most fun. Although I used the plaid as is with the burgundy and brown in the background, for the motifs, I cut it and divided the plaid into three groups: red, yellow/orange, and green. When hooking the leaves, I pulled the green into the green leaves, the red into the red leaves, and the yellow/orange into the purple leaves. I used these three colors again for the pompom flowers.

The most challenging aspect of this rug was its size and the time it takes to hook a very large rug. I learned to pace myself and only hook a manageable amount each week. I was lucky that this pattern had variety, so there was always something interesting to hook.

I was inspired to try rug hooking after hearing about it from a friend I taught with and decided that when I retired, I would give it a try myself. I love the creative aspect of combining colors, types of wool, and techniques.

Cheltenham, 10' x 8', #5- and #8-cut hand-dyed and as-is wool on linen. Designed by Martina Lesar of Martina Lesar Hooked Rug Studio and hooked by Susan Grant, Georgetown, Ontario, Canada, 2016. FISCHBACK PHOTOGRAPHY

Susan Grant
Georgetown, Ontario, Canada

Susan is a retired high school teacher. She's a member of the Ontario Hooking Craft Guild and the Georgetown Rug Hooking Guild. This is her fourth appearance in Celebration.

Ense's Bed Rug

Cindy's classes helped calm my "I can't do this" mindset, and her patience helped me grow so much in color planning and trusting myself to step out of that box we all put ourselves in. As a result, I saw color planning and shading so differently. Looking at this rug as it hangs in our foyer releases a ton of emotions for that season of our lives. As I observe certain leaves and flowers and the days I was working with them, I remember how they represent so many bends in the road at that time.

I chose colors that I enjoy working with. I wanted the rug to have a brilliance to it without oversaturating the piece with color. The spot dyes used throughout in the veins in the leaves and vines created a flow throughout the rug. The outside scalloped edge was my favorite part of the rug. When I hooked it, I felt it brought the rug to a nice place by tying everything together. I think the biggest challenge was using a few colors in eight values and trying to move them around the rug for eye and balance.

I first became interested in rug hooking after I saw a woman in an antique shop hooking a Santa face. With the information she gave me, I found Rebecca Erb in an issue of *Celebration*, and off I went. I feel like rug hooking is so much bigger than the craft itself. As we walk though that ugly word "cancer," it reminds me how shading of leaves and flowers are similar to life's changes. Some days are dark, needing a mixture of light color values to enhance the light that all rugs need. Much like our lives, we grow out of our darkness, and the light becomes much more effective. Rug hooking is so much more than a craft. It introduces you to expression and imagination. This rug is a treasure to our family, and thank you to *Celebration* for shining even more light on it.

Years ago, while I was attending a class taught by Cindy Irwin, she held up this pattern to show our class. I immediately fell in love with it, but I knew it was way over my head at that time.

I must admit, the day I ordered this pattern, the excitement was overwhelming. I started planning how I was going to stretch my learning by using eight values of wool and incorporating shading and spot dyeing.

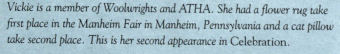

Vickie M. Landis
Mount Joy, Pennsylvania

Vickie is a member of Woolwrights and ATHA. She had a flower rug take first place in the Manheim Fair in Manheim, Pennsylvania and a cat pillow take second place. This is her second appearance in Celebration.

In The Judges' Eyes

Gorgeous; exquisite shading; well-placed colors; harmonious colors and judicious use of outlining.

Ense's Bed Rug, 45" x 56", #3- to 5-cut wool on linen.
Designed by Honey Bee Hive and hooked by Vickie M. Landis, Mount Joy, Pennsylvania, 2016. CINDY IRWIN

Geometric Star

Quilting and rug hooking are two of my favorite hobbies. I can't think of a better design to hook than a quilt pattern. Geometric designs especially speak to me and are my favorite types of rugs to hook.

I usually hook with textured wool, so I decided to use many different pieces of wool in each color family I was working with to make my rug more interesting and quilt-like. I even added some sparkly wool! I thought a lot about what colors to use for this rug. To plan it out, I used colored pencils to fill in a black-and-white version of the design. I made several color plans before deciding which version I'd go with.

It gave me a better idea of what the rug would look like when it was finished. I opted for red, off white, brown, and black in my final color plan. Using brown and black as the background colors made the red and off-white stars shine. I struggle when deciding how bright I want to make a rug. I like rich jewel-tone colors, but I also like fun, bright colors. I opted for a more traditional approach this time around.

The brown squares were a bit challenging since there were so many of them. I looked at how many squares I had to do and tried to come up with a plan to work through them. I thought that I would hook one a day, but one square took quite a while to hook. I

abandoned the idea and just kept at it as time allowed. I was pleased with the way the rug turned out. In fact, I entered it in my hometown fair where it won Best of Show!

I first learned about rug hooking after seeing it at my local fair over 20 years ago. I taught myself how to hook, but it was slow going without the Internet or a teacher to help guide me along. It never ceases to amaze me at how much there is to learn about rug hooking and how much more there is for me to learn. Rug hooking allows each of us to be as creative as we choose to be, which is one of the reasons why I love it so much.

Geometric Star, 45" x 45", #8-cut wool on linen. Designed by Goat Hill
Designs and hooked by Linda Gustafson, Chardon, Ohio, 2016. HEIDI CAMPANY PHOTOGRAPHY

Linda Gustafson
Chardon, Ohio

Linda is a mother and homemaker. She's a member of the Western Reserve Rug Hookers Guild ATHA Chapter #119, the National Guild of Pearl K. McGown Hookcrafters, Buckeye Rugcrafters, the Lorain County Rughookers, and the Buckeye Rug Hooking State Guild. This is her fourth appearance in Celebration.

In The Judges' Eyes

Nice blending of colors; wool selection along with skillful color planning makes this geometric stand out; color choices blend beautifully: an exploding star!

Helen's Tapestry

This particular rug really spoke to me because of my background. I live on a farm, raise animals, and love photographing wildflowers, so this piece embodied many of my interests. I also prefer a fine cut so the images are more distinct. I found the pattern in a catalog from the Harry M. Fraser Co. and decided it would be fun and challenging and met my criteria.

I started the rug in a class at the Holland, Michigan Rug Camp with Anne Bond as my instructor. Anne dyed the background wool for me. I had just started dyeing wool, and Anne coached me in color planning the rest of the project. I wanted vivid colors of various values to make the motifs come alive. The numerous colors and values provided me with the opportunity to sharpen my dyeing skills. The cuts I used were #2 and #3 for the motifs and details, #4 and #5 for the background, and #6 for the accent lines and outer border.

I really like all of the animals. The tiger and the large deer are particular favorites. Each motif became a project of its own to interpret, develop, and hook so that it integrated with the other motifs. The pond proved to be very challenging. I dyed and hooked it three times before I was satisfied. To finish the rug, I sewed a cord into a strip of wool and attached it to the turned edge under the rug.

My wife is a long-time rug hooker. I traveled to Holland, Michigan, with her when she attended rug camp. For five years, I photographed in the area while she was in class. One day in 2012 while visiting her class, Margaret McNamara insisted that I sit down and hook. I really thought that I had no interest in hooking, but after a short time I found hooking to be very enjoyable and rewarding. You can be as creative as you want to be. I especially love rug hooking because it is an activity my wife and I can share. I have signed up for rug hooking camp every year since. *Helen's Tapestry* is my third project.

John Cunningham
Anderson, Indiana

John is a retired engineer who lives on a farm and raises donkeys. He's a member of ATHA, Puckihuddlers in Indianapolis, and the White River Ruggers in Muncie, Indiana. This is his first appearance in Celebration.

In The Judges' Eyes

The detailed photos show expert skill in hooking small motifs; skillful handling of colors.

Helen's Tapestry, 32" x 53½", #2- to 6-cut hand-dyed, over-dyed, and as-is wool on linen.
Designed by Jeanette Szatkowski and hooked by John Cunningham, Anderson, Indiana, 2016.

Larkspur Chintz

My inspiration for the rug is two-fold: my love for #3-cut, fine-shaded design and being able to assist one of my favorite rug hookers, Jasmine Benjamin Robinson, daughter of my teacher, Jeanne Benjamin, with her McGown certification. The color palette was chosen to coordinate with another rug I had hooked. Jasmine helped to color plan and dye the wool. The careful placement of dark to light in the leaves, coupled with the pops of color in the blues and purples of the flowers, gives the rug depth. The motif literally jumps off the background.

We used a black/green background (Jeanne named it "Barb's Forest Green" after me) and chose two 6-value green swatches and a 6-value green-to-blue swatch to give the leaves life, dimension, and energy. Spot dyes were used for the pale green leaves, berries, and stems for some added interest. The 6-value blue and purple-to-blue swatches add the needed contrast to all of the cool greens. I loved the medium values of blue and green in the border the most. This wasn't the first choice when choosing colors, but it brought the whole rug together. Bringing these colors from the motif to the "frame" provided cohesiveness to the piece.

The frond leaves were the most challenging to hook. I didn't want to get too light too quickly, working from the bottom to the top of each one. When working on a fine-shaded piece, I find it helpful to put the rug on the floor and stand back. That way, I can gain the proper perspective on foreground to background, how the shadows are playing out, and more.

Every rug has been a learning experience, and with at least 25 rugs completed, I've learned a lot. This rug could easily have been a study in green. Keeping all of the green interesting and lively while adding the warm purple and cooler blue was an education in color placement and challenged my fine shading skills. This is the first time I've used this type of frame border, bringing "interior" colors to the "outside," and the effect was striking.

I first learned about rug hooking on television, and soon after, I spotted an ad in our local paper for a one-day workshop with Jeanne Benjamin. That was in 1991, and Jeanne has been my teacher now for over 25 years. Before I retired, I used to call rug hooking "my sanity." My hands like to be busy and painting with wool relaxes me while stretching my creative ability. I love to watch each piece take on a life of its own.

Barbara Granlund
Hardwick, Massachusetts

Barbara is a retired Vice President and Director of Human Resources for a local bank. Larkspur Chintz won first prize in the 253rd Hardwick Fair in 2016 and was shown at the Caraway Rug School show in 2016. She is a member of ATHA.

In The Judges' Eyes

Very nicely done; beautiful colors; exquisite; unusual shading of leaves and vibrant color plan make this rug a standout.

Larkspur Chintz, 27" x 43½", #3-cut hand-dyed wool on monk's cloth.
Designed by Jane McGown Flynn and hooked by Barbara Granlund, Hardwick, Massachusetts, 2016. JEREMIAH BENJAMIN

Nagari

I was awestruck by Judy Carter's "Eye See You" display at the Sauder Village Rug Week in 2012 and immediately signed up for her next available class on hooking realistic animals. The tiger pattern was my pick for the class.

This was my first venture into textured wools. Textures provided new ways to create realistic color variations in the tiger's hair than I would have otherwise created just using spot or value-dyed wools. This mix of textures best represented the natural coloring of the subject piece.

Creating depth in the muzzle area took extra effort and care since I needed to closely study the photo from which the

pattern was adapted. The extra effort was worth it, though—I was pleased with the way the piece turned out. My favorite section of the piece though had to be the tiger's eyes. I love the way they express an attitude that says you don't want to mess with him! I finished the rug with a simple whipped edge that frames the rug without distracting from the main subject.

Nagari debuted at the Virginia Rugfest in Mechanicsville, Virginia, this past April, and I'm looking forward to its next appearance during Rug Week at Sauder Village. While this rug proved to be a challenge for me, I'm thankful for how it allowed me to grow in my craft.

When I was young, I loved doing art in school, but eventually, I had to make a choice and decided to pursue a career in engineering instead. My wife, Susi, has been hooking for about 25 years, and after attending many events with her through the years, I finally decided to join in on the fun. Rug hooking has allowed me to rekindle my creative and artistic interests. I have made some patterns for fellow hookers, and when time allows, I even work on my own stained glass projects. I retired this past fall, and I'm looking forward to getting to spend more time hooking and designing rugs as well as finishing up some unfinished projects.

Nagari, 21½" x 21½", #3- to 5-cut textured wool on rug warp.
Designed by Leonard Feenan, adapted from a picture taken by Judy Carter, and hooked by Dennis Seyller,
Chesapeake, Virginia, 2016. JEANNE KLINK

Dennis Seyller
Chesapeake, Virginia

Denny is recently retired and is looking forward to future rug hooking projects. He's a member of the James River Rug Hookers in Chuckatuck, Virginia, and the Shockoe Slip Rug Hookers in Richmond, Virginia. This is his second appearance in Celebration.

In The Judges' Eyes

Eyes are engaging; excellent shading; you can feel the stare of the tiger.

Neville Sisters 1764

I wanted to create this rug to challenge myself. I gravitate toward primitive-style hooking, so it was exciting to utilize shading and detail with such a large pattern in a small cut. Because I was hooking in a #4 cut, I knew I had to dye very specifically to achieve the effect I wanted.

When choosing the colors for the piece, I wanted colors that were warm and appealing to my eye. My home is filled with antiques, so I wanted to make sure this piece would fit into that aesthetic. I dyed all of the wool in this rug myself. I found that dip dyes worked wonderfully for the leaves and flowers.

Going from warm yellows into deep reds was a wonderful exercise in controlling colors to achieve a perfect piece of wool. Dyeing wool is such an exciting process. I love everything about it and can't imagine not dyeing my own wool!

I absolutely love how some of the flowers turned out. My favorite piece of wool was dyed a deep yellow that merged into a deep red—perfect for flower petals. I was most surprised at how difficult the border was. My teacher, Sue Clark, and I colored numerous mock-ups to try to find the right color combinations. I hooked (and unhooked!) many variations before finding what finally felt right. Hooking this rug taught me how to balance color throughout the rug and to keep trying various color layouts until the perfect combination comes together.

I first got started in rug hooking after seeing a rug hooking demonstration in Springfield, Massachusetts. As soon as I saw it, I knew this was a craft I wanted to learn. Rug hooking satisfies my need to create something that makes me smile. All of the phases of rug hooking, from designing patterns to dyeing wool and being part of a community of kindred spirts, fill me with such joy. I love wool in all its forms. In fact, I'm also teaching myself how to knit.

Jennifer Grahovac
Wooster, Ohio

Jennifer and her husband have a small organic farm in Ohio. She's a member of ATHA and the Fort Lauren's Rugcrafters Guild in Ohio. She's won two Best of Show awards for two different rugs at county fairs in Ohio and Minnesota.

In The Judges' Eyes

Perfect shading of border ribbons; stylistic flowers and leaves hooked in a dramatic but simple fashion; light and playful.

Neville Sisters 1764, 28" x 49", #4-cut hand-dyed wool on rug warp.
Designed by Jane McGown Flynn and hooked by Jennifer Grahovac, Wooster, Ohio, 2016. SHARON DOYLE

Octopus

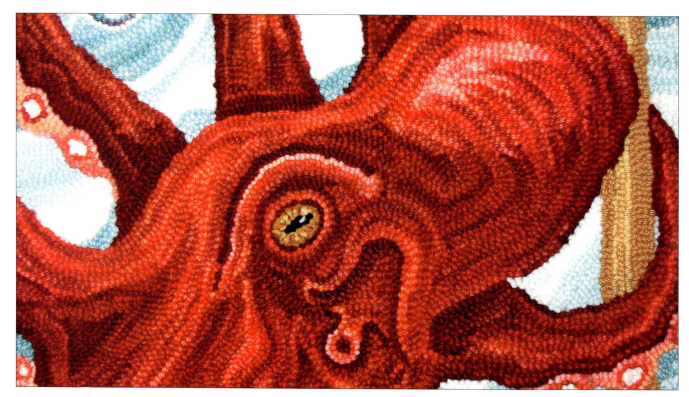

My kids and I were making a papier-mâché octopus as a prop for a play, and I loved the shape of them: all sensuous curving lines, circles, and glorious colors. We did some research and discovered that they are intelligent, capable of solving problems and using tools, and have three hearts with blue blood. I was so fascinated and couldn't stop thinking how fun it would be to design and hook.

I'm a punch hooker, and I love hooking with my rug yarns. I chose a finer 3-ply rug yarn for a refined look and even finer 2-ply yarn for the background to enhance the look of flowing water.

I love brick reds and rich, dark oranges; they are delicious to work with, and when they're set against light turquoise/tealish blue, it makes my soul sing! I dyed a couple of reddish orange skeins with a gentle variegation technique, and each had different values to them. The underside of the tentacle needed to be much lighter, and I wanted a translucent glow to them, so before the dye was all absorbed in my pot, I added another skein, and it created

the lovely pinky hue. I added a little yellow to increase the glow and give it a bit more variation and tie it into the yellow frame. I used similar dye techniques for the water colors—three gently variegated skeins that were all similar colors but had different values in them, plus one white.

The background was the most challenging part. I didn't have the color right a couple of times and once had the water flowing in the wrong direction. I felt it didn't lead the eye around the piece properly. Each time I got some of the backing in, I would look at it in the mirror or would take pictures and then change the

pictures to black and white or rotate it. This helped me get a better feel of what wasn't working, so I could pull it out and start again.

I got started in rug hooking after finding an old *Celebration* book in the library. I loved the look of the rugs, did some research, and was enthralled with the process of punch hooking. My husband wanted to try it too, so we bought supplies together, drew our own patterns, and punched our first rugs. After just a few loops, I was totally hooked! I loved it so much that I wanted to teach it too, and I'm now a certified Oxford instructor.

Simone Vojvodin
Parkhill, Ontario, Canada

Simone is an artist, proprietor, teacher, and homeschooling mother. She has a rug shop called Red Maple Ruggery where she creates and sells patterns, rug hooking yarns and wools, and rug hooking supplies. This is her fourth appearance in Celebration.

Octopus, 33" x 37½", 2-ply and 3-ply hand-dyed wool yarn on monk's cloth.
Designed and hooked by Simone Vojvodin, Parkhill, Ontario, Canada, 2016.

Bold color enhances the mystery; great directional shading; magnificent bubbles and tentacles; diagonal water suggests upward movement; nice blending of several colors.

Old World Santa

and even had a beautiful stand crafted for him. Because I wanted him to be a dummy board, I finished the edge along his outline. It was challenging since there aren't any straight lines! I sewed the edges to the inside and sewed a flexible rug tape over that. I followed that up with a thick pellon layer to give the piece more stability, and I put on a wool backing over that. I then attached it to the dummy board using Velcro.

The face was the most challenging part of the rug for me. But, with the guidance of Victoria Hart Ingalls, I was able to stay calm and get through it. Her patience and confidence in my ability helped me tremendously. When it comes to finishing a uniquely shaped piece like this, I know that trusting my instincts will lead me in the right direction.

This past August, *Old World Santa* won a blue ribbon for fine cut and the sweepstakes for rugs at the 2016 Minnesota State Fair. I also won a blue ribbon in the Wide Cut Over 3 Feet category at the 2016 Minnesota State Fair.

I am fairly new to fine hooking, and after hooking this piece, I discovered that I want to do more. I have always loved hooked rugs and took my first class with Kathy Morton. She was, and still is, a great inspiration to me and is the reason I continued hooking after that first class. I love the whole process from picking or designing a pattern to color planning to hooking and finishing. I love discovering the power of color. I never hesitate to take out colors that aren't working and finding the ones that do. That's the joy of the craft for me, and I wouldn't have it any other way. While I have dyed my own wool, I haven't done so extensively, so that's the next challenge I'm looking to tackle.

I was excited to start on this project because I love everything about Christmas and Santas. Christmas pieces lend themselves well to the use of bright colors. The toys, in particular, were so much fun to hook because I got to use so many different colors. It was a delight to find a way to make it all "work."

In order to best place him on display, I decided to make him into a "dummy board"

Sallie Skinner
Wayzata, Minnesota
Sallie works with a wish-granting organization for children with chronic or terminally ill conditions and tutors children with Down syndrome at Gigi's Playhouse. This is her second appearance in Celebration.

In The Judges' Eyes

Exquisite shading; perfection; sweet well-done Santa. Striking color makes the elements crisp.

Old World Santa, 19" x 39½", #3- and #5-cut wool on monk's cloth.
Designed by Victoria Hart Ingalls and color planned and hooked by Sallie Skinner, Wayzata, Minnesota, 2016. ANNIE MARIE PHOTOGRAPHY

Say Cheese

When I saw this pattern, it just screamed for colors and designs. I love playing with color, and I've always liked the line of fabrics by designer Laurel Burch, so I was eager to get started. Most of the noodles of wool I used in this rug were leftovers—pieces from friends' projects that weren't substantial enough to use again or leftovers from my (failed) attempts at shading. Some wool was off-the-bolt or recycled. I used the colors I liked the best and the amount needed for the space, which was so much fun. The more colors, the better! If I didn't have enough of one color, I added something else to it to make it work.

I loved making the designs on the actual cats, whether I was making them up as I went along or trying something new. The plaids, in particular, were fun, though I also loved the stripes, polka dots, and the couple of "shaded" cats. I wanted every cat to be different, so it wouldn't become monotonous.

The hardest part was working in a #3 cut. I really had to pay attention to making those loops and not overpacking as I hooked. In the past, I typically hooked in a #8 cut or sometimes a #6 cut. A #3 cut is a lot smaller! It took a lot of patience in the beginning. When I finished the rug, I just rolled the backing forward and whipped with yarn. It's nice because when you're done, you're done. There's no need for rug tape.

There was a time when I would have doubted whether I could hook in a #3 cut, but this rug gave me confidence that I could. It may not have wonderfully shaded scrolls or beautifully shaded flowers or fruits, but I love my finished product. I will forever be in awe of my talented friends who not only have the skill, but the patience for a shaded #3-cut floral, room-sized rug. I am so glad they encouraged me to do this rug.

Rug hooking is such an expressive art. The first time I ever picked up a hook was at the state fair. The local guild was demonstrating, and they let me and my daughters try it out. I couldn't wait to get my own tools: the stripper, the frame, and a hook. I knew I needed to do this. That was about 12–13 years ago, and I've been hooking ever since.

Say Cheese, 39½"x 31½", #3- and #4-cut new and recycled wool on linen. Designed by Christine Little from Encompassing Designs and hooked by Rhonda Bateman, Glen Rock, Pennsylvania, 2016. IMPACT XPOZURES

Rhonda Bateman
Glen Rock, Pennsylvania

Rhonda is a mother to three teenagers and a preschool teacher to 3- and 4-year-olds. She's a member of the Woolwrights Rug Guild in Pennsylvania and the Mason Dixon Rug Hookers in Maryland. This is her first appearance in Celebration.

In The Judges' Eyes

Lovely interpretation; adorable; cats from plaid to purple and everything in between.

Spirits of the Lake

I took great pleasure and inspiration designing this rug based on the beloved loons I see on Lake Potanipo in New Hampshire where we have a home. I combined traditional hooking and Waldoboro techniques with hand-dyed and fused wools (hand-dyed wool fused together with a shiny fabric), as well as novelty fabrics (such as metallics) and yarns. When I designed my piece, I looked for different materials that would give texture to the birds and shiny fibers to enhance the fish or water. It was this creative combination of fibers that really gave life to the piece.

I like to use wool with a range of light to dark values. For this piece in particular, I used dyed wool with three colors blended together to give the piece movement and interest. My favorite part of hooking this rug was creating the center loon with his wings back where I was able to add a lot of texture. I wanted to achieve a shiny, wet look, and using velvet fabric on the loons' heads

brought that aesthetic across. To finish the rug, I sewed a black wool edge around the finished piece and then attached it to a wood frame.

This rug taught me so much about the challenge of designing and hooking a large composition and making it come together

well. I enjoy so much about the art of rug hooking. It allows me to experiment with many different fibers to create different aesthetics. It's easy to change anything you've hooked to get exactly the look you want. And as an art teacher, I love that I can take the project with me to work!

Sandra Grant
Brookline, New Hampshire

Sandra is an artist and art teacher. She won the Viewer's Choice Award at the Hooked in the Mountains exhibit. She's a member of ATHA and the Green Mountain Rug Hooking Guild. This is her second appearance in Celebration.

In The Judges' Eyes

Artful use of materials; I like the addition of real feathers; the velour works well in this piece.

I originally had a weaving business that I had to give up due to shoulder injuries. I was looking for another craft and discovered rug hooking. I've been doing that ever since. I enjoy the creative process, starting from an idea or vision, drawing that idea on the backing, and hooking it to completion. I love to work with bright colors from hand-dyed wools. And I especially love adding textures and different materials to make the piece come alive. Rug hooking gives me the great satisfaction of being an artist, and I'm thrilled to have found this craft.

Spirits of the Lake, 51" x 26", #3- and #4-cut hand-dyed and fused wools (some hoved), velours, metallics, yarns, and feathers on linen. Designed and hooked by Sandra Grant, Brookline, New Hampshire, 2016.

ANNE-MARIE LITTENBERG

The Conspiracy

I really enjoy David Galchutt's art. It's so different than what I usually create—I tend to hook rugs of shaded florals. There's so much color and whimsy in David's art, which I find delightful. This is the second piece I've made from an adaptation of his work—my first adaptation, *Hoot*, can be found in *Celebration 26*—and both of them were so much fun to do. I'm keeping my eye on number three now.

I began creating this rug during a three-day class I took with Pris Buttler, and that really helped me get off to a great start. When I adapt a piece from an artist, I try to stay as close to the artist's color choices as I can. After all, that's one of the features that

drew my attention in the first place! I did not, however, hook the pears in green like in the original painting, but instead, I chose a combination of reds, greens, and browns, which I created through dip dyeing and spot dyeing.

My favorite part about this rug is the facial expressions of the couple. It was tricky to capture the mischievous look in their eyes, but I'm so pleased with the way it turned out. Of course, there's always one area that poses a challenge. Mine was getting the hook in her nose just right. I must have put it in and taken it out at least twenty times before getting it exactly how I wanted it, and I'm pleased with the way it

ended up. I finished the rug by creating a border with a double row of whipping.

I've been involved with fiber arts for many years. I had quilted for twenty years along with reupholstering furniture and practicing needlepoint and tapestry. After quilting for so long, I found I couldn't hand sew anymore, so I needed to find another hobby to keep me busy. I came upon a group of ladies at a street fair back in 1999 who were hooking rugs, and the rest is history. I find hooking very relaxing. I love trying out different dye formulas and seeing what I can create to use in my next project since I dye all my wool myself.

The Conspiracy, 38" x 38", #3-cut wool on monk's cloth. Adapted from a painting by David Galchutt and hooked by Marion Sachs, York, Pennsylvania, 2016. IMPACT XPOZURES

Marion Sachs
York, Pennsylvania

Marion has been retired for many years. She's a member of ATHA and the Pearl McGown Conestoga Group in Lancaster, Pennsylvania. This is her fifth rug to appear in Celebration.

Vibrant interpretation; every detail is done well; amazing artistry; master technique.

The Queen's Desire

I loved the floral center of this piece the most with its great variety of color. The array of reds, blues, and yellows played well off each other. Nancy C. Blood helped me with the color planning. The most challenging section was dealing with the abundant scrolls. They were the first scrolls I had ever hooked. I was lucky to have a great teacher, Peg Hannum, affectionately known as the "Queen of Scrolls," to offer me guidance. With her inspiration, nothing was too challenging. This rug taught me about perseverance and how important it is to keep hooking, even during trickier spots, because the end result is all worth it.

You don't even want to know how I got started with rug hooking! I was never interested in learning this art form. However, fifteen years ago, I offered to drive my non-driving friend to day-long classes at Peg Hannum's home—about an hour's drive each way. Rather than sit idly all day, I decided to try hooking. For a whole year, I worked on a small chair seat and got "hooked." I actually hooked my first rug at the age of 75.

Helen B. Lynch
Glenmoore, Pennsylvania

Helen is a retired mathematics teacher. She belongs to the Brandywine and Woolwright chapters of ATHA and the Conestoga chapter of McGown. This is her third appearance in Celebration.

In The Judges' Eyes

Nice color; an opus! masterful shading from ribbon turns to carnation edges; colors of scrolls adds great interest; nicely hooked ribbon; crisp color contrast.

The Queen's Desire, 46" x 80", #3-cut wool on linen.
Designed by Pearl McGown and hooked by Helen B. Lynch, Glenmoore, Pennsylvania, 2016. IMPACT EXPOSURES

"Sleep Walker"

I adapted my rug from an original painting by George Lindmark. I fell in love with the emotion and movement in the piece and was compelled to try to recreate that in a hooked rug. Drawing the portrait itself on the backing material is always a challenge. If I don't get it right at that point, then there's no sense continuing!

Once the drawing is done, then it's a matter of finding the right colors. Skin tones and skin shading were very challenging and took a lot of trial and error. (Luckily I have quite a good selection of skin tones and other colors in my stash!) I must have hooked and pulled out some sections at least eight times. When I'd hook a particularly challenging section and felt unsure about it,

I would leave it overnight and approach it again fresh the next day to see if I'd need to re-do it.

I prefer hooking with wool yarn rather than wool strips. I love everything about hooking with yarn from the vast array of available colors and textures to the way it feels as it moves across my hand. I chose the backing from my stash because of the fineness of the material at 400 holes per square inch. It allowed me to create more detail than would have been possible had I used a more standard backing like linen or burlap. Since the backing was very fine, I had to unravel the yarns into one or two strands and separated the roving into the thickness needed in order to fit.

I have always been involved in fiber art in some form or another, making quilts, dolls, animals, teddy bears, counted cross stitch, knitting, and sewing. But when I discovered rug hooking in 2010 after seeing an exhibition at Upper Canada Village, I knew I was "hooked"! Not only did it allow for use of all sorts of colors and textures, but it also allowed for artistic expression that I found similar to painting, as though I was "painting" with the wool. Rug hooking is such a creative outlet that completely relaxes me, and I love everything about it.

Susan J. Baker
Stanbridge East, Quebec, Canada

Susan is a retired research scientist. She's a member of the Brome County Rug Hookers. She entered Celebration for the first time last year, and her rug, Greta Garbo, was selected as the cover.

"Sleep Walker", 20½" x 16½", wool yarn and roving with small amounts of cotton yarn hooked through unidentified material (probably cotton). Adapted from a painting by George Lindmark and hooked by Susan J. Baker, Stanbridge East, Quebec, Canada, 2016. TONY PEIRCE

In The Judges' Eyes

Superb shading that lets the expression shine through, technically flawless; good natural balance of colors.

Dos Caballos

Dos Caballos ("two horses" in Spanish) was started during a Multicolores rug hooking trip to Guatemala led by Mary Anne Wise. During this wonderful, inspiring trip, we hooked alongside women who have become master hookers. They taught us their particular approach to hooking, which is deeply influenced by the rich handwoven textile heritage of Guatemala.

At the introduction to our hooking buddies, we were seated on the lawn of a hotel on the shores of Lake Atitlan. A gorgeous red textile piece with stylized horses caught my attention as it rippled in the breeze. This was the piece on which I based my design. The horses are made in a weft pick-up brocade design, woven on a back strap loom. As a weaver, I was in awe of the technical proficiency to produce such

a piece. Later in the market at Chichicastenango, I saw several other variations on the motif, all woven in the brilliant saturated palette of most Guatemalan textiles.

For materials to hook our pieces, we headed to the local village market by tuk-tuks (small 2 or 3 person taxis on a motorcycle), where there was a paca (used clothing) dealer. Each piece of clothing cost the equivalent of about 20 cents, and we

Sara Judith
Nelson, British Columbia

*Sara started hooking after purchasing a kit at
Deanne Fitzpatrick's studio. She is a hooking
teacher accredited by Amy Oxford, helps
organize Prairie Harvest Rug Hooking School
and Puget South Rug School, and is a member
of TIGHR, FAN, and several rug hooking
guilds in Canada. She has appeared in previous
editions of* Celebration.

In The Judges' Eyes

*First rate folk art adaptation; bold colors are
well balanced with skillful shading; use of warm
and cool colors adds dimension to piece.*

Dos Caballos, 50½" x 27½", hand-cut
recycled T-shirt material (mainly cotton) on
monk's cloth. Adapted from a Guatemalan
woven textile and designed and hooked
by Sara Judith, Nelson, British Columbia,
Canada, 2016.

chose clothing based on what was suitable
for our hooking. Back at our tables we
learned to cut off hems and seams, fold the
T-shirt fabric and cut by hand across the
grain, in most cases, a thumb's width. The
T-shirts were mainly brightly colored, but
we also learned to value patterned ones
that gave mottled or textured effects.

In my piece, I particularly like the *ikat*
effect, which is found in many Guatemalan textiles. The warp yarns are bound in
a particular sequence for resistance before
dyeing and prior to weaving. I was able
to mimic this effect by using a red T-shirt
striped with white, which I had to space
out to balance the rug.

The two horses were separated by a
randa, the band of embroidery used to join
cloth panels. The diamond patterning was
fun as colors played with each other. As

with a Guatemalan piece of woven cloth,
there is no formal border. I finished the
edge of the rug by whipping with a strip of
T-shirt material.

Dos Caballos travels proudly with me to
rug hooking events. When home, it lives
on top of an ancient chest in my dining
room.

Fairy Fantasia

The inspiration for this rug came from an enchanting illustration from a children's book called *The Little Green Road to Fairyland* by Ida Rentoul Outhwaite, published in 1922. In the story, the fairy is questing to return from the mortal world to Fairyland after relinquishing fairyhood for human form. The frog and the fairy sitting on rocks in a pond, talking to each other, was taken almost directly from the illustration with a few slight modifications. They were both such a delight to hook, and they really came to life for me quickly.

The rug is hooked mainly in wool, but I did utilize some mixed media. For example, the small, delicate leaves and branches in the tree were hooked in yarn; the fairy wings were hooked in a shimmery gossamer fabric and outlined with a narrow silk-like cording; flowers in the fairy's hair and on her dress were mini satin-ribbon floral appliques; and finally, the dragonflies were hooked in a combination of the same gossamer fabric used in the fairy wings but in a different color, along with a satin ribbon outlining and iridescent beaded threading for the body.

When my mother-in-law, Marjorie Gilbert Anderson, whose Peter Rabbit rug appeared in *Celebration II* in 1992, encouraged me to start rug hooking again a few years ago, I said I could not see myself ever wanting to get involved in dyeing! However, by my second rug, she was instructing me on dyeing, and I am particularly proud of the fact that I personally dyed nearly 100% of the wool used in *Fairy Fantasia*. Dyeing techniques used in this rug included straight dyeing, marbling, and spot dyeing—all of which I had previously done—as well as dip dyeing, gradation dyeing, and painting the background sky—techniques I tried for the first time.

For the fairy, frog, and rocks, I stayed fairly close to the colors in the illustration aside from brightening the fairy and frog. In the original illustration, the pond and the sky were in shades of greens and browns, but I envisioned a much more colorful, magical, fantastical background, which led me to the naming, *Fairy Fantasia*—referring to something possessing unreal qualities.

I love every aspect of hooking from creating patterns to dyeing wool to the actual hooking itself. It is both relaxing and stimulating while challenging and stretching my creativity. I continuously marvel at creations by all rug hookers, and I always take away some inspiration in terms of design, color, or technique.

Jane Anderson
Clinton Township, New Jersey

Jane first started rug hooking in the 1980s and picked it up again a few years ago at the encouragement of her mother-in-law. She is the secretary of the Hunterdon County Rug Artisan Guild in Flemington, NJ, and is an ATHA member. This is her first rug featured in Celebration.

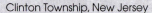
In The Judges' Eyes

Delightful; judicious use of embellishments; pleasing color plan.

Fairy Fantasia, 37" x 23½", #2- to #10- cut wool, primarily personally hand-dyed wool; plus some as-is wool, yarn, beaded thread, ribbon, shimmery organza-type material, and flower embellishments on linen. Adapted from a book illustrated by Ida Rentoul Outhwaite and hooked by Jane Anderson, Clinton Township, New Jersey, 2016.

Harmony on the Pond

I love Dover adult coloring book publications, and when I saw this design, I immediately thought it would make a great hooked rug pattern. My teacher Sibyl Osicka from Ohio color planned this rug for me at the Maryland Shores Rug Hooking School. I did take some artistic liberties to make it a sunset sky instead of a blue sky and using a different swatch for the yellow lilies to match the yellow koi a little better. With this rug, I learned that it's okay to have a teacher do your color planning and not to be afraid to change a color if I like something else better.

I used #3-cut wool so that I could get better detailing into this design, especially with the hummingbird being a large motif with lots of little feathers and details. I also hand-painted a large piece of natural off-white wool for the sunset sky. My four-year-old granddaughter, Kendall, helped me brush the dye onto the natural colored wool out on our patio. She decided that since she helped with this sky that this rug belongs to her when she has a home of her own. (We call it the "Kendall/Mom Mom Rug.")

The most challenging section was the large amount of strap leaves that needed to be done with the fingering technique, which I hate to do. I decided to try an unorthodox method and shade them vertically. (That would probably upset some teachers, but it worked for me!) The rug was finished with three rows of whipping over cotton cording. Because the motifs changed around all four edges, I couldn't just do three solid colors all the way around, which meant that the whipped edge also had to change colors in spots. Once that was done, I sewed cotton rug tape around the back on all four sides by sewing the top of the tape to the backing, the bottom, and then through the middle to secure the center, so it wouldn't twist or move.

I love to create things. I found that rug hooking gave me many different ways to be creative through pattern design, color planning, fabric choices, commercial pattern choices or original designs, dyeing wool with formula choices, and the option to take classes with different kinds of teachers at workshops around the country. I love the challenges of each project and having the satisfaction of seeing a project through to completion.

Harmony on the Pond, 65" x 45", #3-cut hand-dyed wool on rug warp. Adapted with permission from a coloring book by Dover Books and hooked by Sharon A. Kollman, Glen Arm, Maryland, 2016.

Sharon A. Kollman
Glen Arm, Maryland

Sharon became interested in rug hooking after seeing a round bunny rug at the Maryland State Fair in 1997 and found a local teacher, Marguerite Hastings (who will be 102 in December and is still hooking rugs), to introduce her to the art. She is a member of the Mason Dixon Chapter of ATHA in Maryland and has won her club's award for "Best in the Fine Cut Division of Rug Hooking."

Overall well-executed adaptation; spectacular colors in the feathers; crisp shading captures the stark moment.

Iron Workers Eating Lunch on a Beam

My husband, David, is an iron worker, and every iron worker knows the picture *Iron Workers Eating on a Bean* by Charles Ebbets. I designed and created this rug around this photograph as a dedication to him and his profession.

I knew I didn't want to hook the top part of the famed picture because it has a lot of atmospheric perspective, so I chose another photograph, *Old Fisher Body Plant* by Jennifer Underwood, to integrate on top to show the changes of the industry. I knew I wanted bright fabrics to offset the black-and-white portion of the rug to bring it a little more life. What drew me to the photograph was how dirty and run down the plant was contrasted against the bright vibrancy of the graffiti.

I changed the wording of the graffiti to reflect more personal messages. I added my husband's name; Local 86—Seattle, Washington, the local he began his career in; Local 25—Detroit, Michigan, the local where he is finishing his career; and my initials along with the initials of both photographers. I also took out one of the iron workers and added my husband to the rug. He's the one in color, looking out at the *Old Fisher Body Plant* part of the rug. The past is in black and white while the color portions represent the present.

I tried to match the colors of both photographs as closely as I could. Anne Bond of Visions of Ewe did the dyeing and color planning for me. I wanted to use the color to show depth in the rug, and I think was most successful in the upper left corner.

The most challenging part of making this rug was getting the buildings right, especially

the windows. At first, I left open spaces for the windows and then added them in after I finished the building, but I found it much faster and easier to start cutting the wool out to add the windows in.

With rug hooking, I love the balance of freedom and constraints. I have the freedom to create a rug on any topic I want, but I still have the constraint of needing to find exactly the right wool I need for it. When I look at a piece of wool, I never know what piece it'll be part of until I'm cutting it up and start hooking it in!

Tina M. Mikols
Livonia, Michigan

Tina started rug hooking from kits 20 years ago. She started taking rug hooking classes six years ago after meeting Anne Bond at an art show in Novi, Michigan. This is her first rug featured in Celebration.

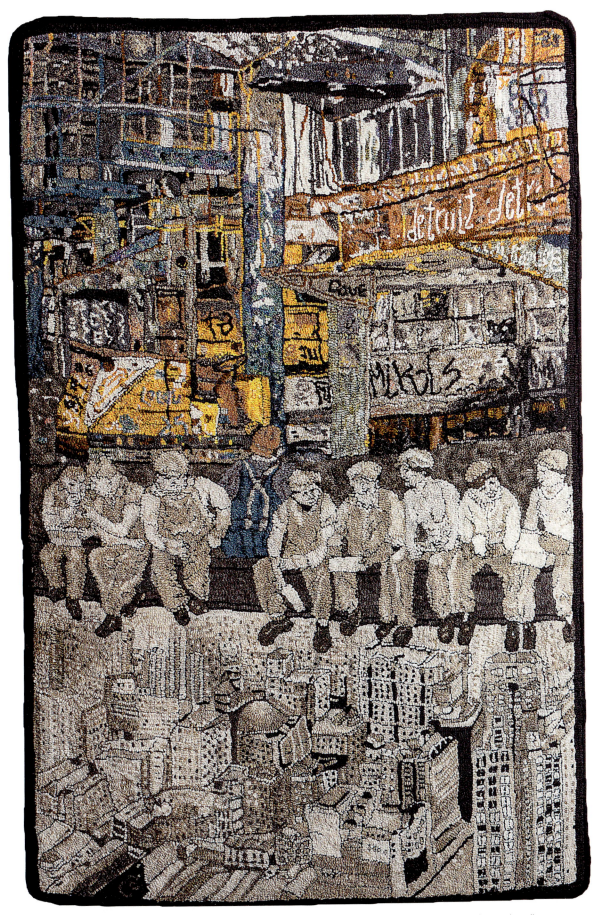

Iron Workers Eating Lunch on a Beam, 26" x 40", #3- to 5-cut hand-dyed and as-is wool on linen.
Adapted with permission from photographs by Charles Ebbets and Jennifer Underwood and designed and
hooked by Tina Mikols, Livonia, Michigan, 2016. ANDREA LYNNE PHOTOGRAPHY

Luncheon of the Boating Party

My love of impressionistic painters shone through once again with this adaptation of Renoir's famed painting, *Luncheon of the Boating Party*. So far, I've hooked adaptations of paintings by Monet, Seurat, and Renoir, and I look forward to hooking more in the future. (Who's next? Degas? Manet?)

I prefer using rug warp as a backing and 100% wool. Except for my use of some "as is" plaids, all of the wool used was dyed for previous rugs. I did not dye any wool specifically for this rug. Dyeing methods included straight, dip, spot, and 8 value. I began dyeing my own wool six months after learning to rug hook. I love trying different colors and dyeing techniques. It's lots of fun to spend an afternoon experimenting and then using what I create in a rug.

The people's faces were definitely the most difficult part of this rug. I began by doing the faces and some of the hats. I knew it would be a challenging rug, and it didn't disappoint me. Capturing the right coloring and expression of each of the party attendees was quite a challenge. I had to reverse hook several of the faces many times. They just didn't seem to capture the right expressions. I learned about patience, patience, patience when hooking detail. I would become anxious to finish a person or section but found that rushing didn't work. Paying attention to the smallest bit of color or detail paid off in the end, and thank goodness for Diane Stoffel's help and encouragement while attending Caraway Rug School in 2016!

Over the years, I have enjoyed doing cross-stitch, embroidery, crocheting, and knitting. I majored in Art Education in college and have worked with oils, watercolors, pen/ink, and making etched prints. I learned how to make pine needle baskets from a fellow rug hooker and now sell baskets at local craft shows. What I love most about rug hooking though is that it's relaxing, creative, challenging, and just plain fun!

Luncheon of the Boating Party is my tenth rug to appear in *Celebration*. I am always appreciative and thankful for being selected with so many talented fiber artists.

Luncheon of the Boating Party, 27" x 20", #3- to 6-cut hand-dyed and as-is wool on rug warp. Adapted from a painting by Renoir and hooked by Karen Whidden, Southern Pines, North Carolina, 2016. JOHN WHIDDEN

Karen Whidden
Southern Pines, North Carolina

Karen became interested in rug hooking when she and her husband retired to Southern Pines, North Carolina in September 2003. She's a member of ATHA and the Sandhills Rug Artists (SRA) in Southern Pines. This is her tenth appearance in Celebration.

Excellent rendition of a classic; incredible detail with great feeling; looks like a good party.

Narragansett Towers

When my daughter was preparing to get married, I asked her and her fiancé what they would like me to rug hook for them. They asked if I could hook the Towers, which was the location of their wedding. They actually stood upon the rug during the ceremony! Since they were getting married in December, I wanted to set the rug as a winter scene. While I had taken pictures of the structure myself, I found a wonderful photograph by Duke Marcoccio online, and he gave his permission to use his image as the inspiration for my rug.

Because I adapted this from a photograph, the color selection was relatively easy since there was no need to color plan. For the most part, I chose colors that would be found in nature, but I did use lavender in the stonework to help complement the snow.

While the windblown snow on the building and windows was difficult, the bigger challenge was hooking the heart with the initials. I wanted it to appear as though someone had walked through the snow to create the image. I wound up reworking the heart a few times to get the desired colors and shape, and the end result came close to achieving what I had imagined. I finished the rug by a simple turn of the rug to the top and whipped the edge with handy-dyed yarn from Judith Hotchkiss.

My sister Debra and I started rug hooking about 10 years ago with Jackye Hansen during a week of "sister time" when we were in Maine. I'm also a partner in the Seaside Rug Hooking Company. I have the wonderful privilege of being in business there with my sister who dyes the wool and designs pattern. While my mother and sister are quite artistic, I have difficulty drawing anything other than a stick figure! I am able to use rug hooking as my outlet for "painting."

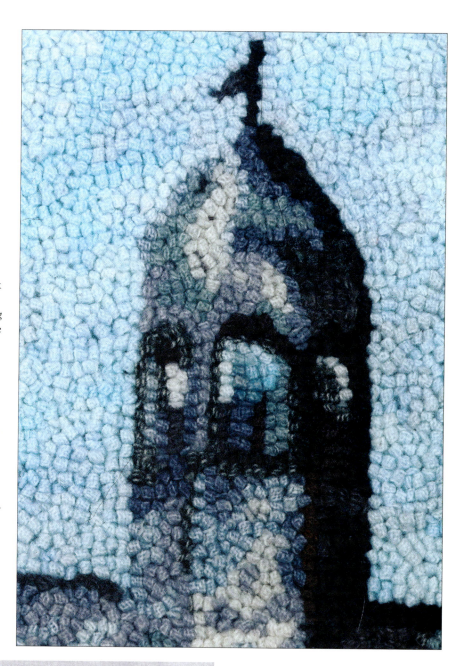

Laura K. Kenyon
South Kingstown, Rhode Island

Laura teaches rug hooking part-time in Rhode Island. Her rug, Blue Moon, was selected for Celebration and won an award at the Northern Teachers Workshop. She is a member of the National Guild of Pearl K. McGown Hookrafters, ATHA, Little Rhode Thrummers, and Green Mountain Rug Hooking Guild.

In The Judges' Eyes

The artist achieved depth using a limited color palette; buildings look great; bold colors create the icy effect; dramatic.

Narragansett Towers, 49" x 28", #3-cut hand-dyed and as-is wool on linen. Adapted from a photo by Duke Marcoccio and hooked by Laura Kenyon, South Kingstown, Rhode Island, 2016. RON COWIE

Nick@Night

I always swore I would never hook portraits of my sons, but my eldest son, Nick, shared a photo of himself that had been taken by a friend, and it was so good, I had to turn it into a rug. (Never say never!) Nick lives, works, and hangs out in our hometown of Dayton, Ohio. He's very active in the community, and I wanted to show how much a part of the downtown that he is.

This meant creating a ghosted image of the skyline that runs through Nick's profile. It wasn't enough to have him simply standing in front of the city; he needed to be part of it. I drew up his portrait and then drew the skyline on a separate piece of tracing paper. I positioned the skyline so it would be visible but not interfere with Nick's face. The beard was the trickiest part because I wanted to create a translucency by mixing the organic texture of his beard with the architectural structures. To finish the rug, I rolled the edge over ⁵⁄₁₆" cotton cording and whipped it with wool yarn I dyed to match.

I always hook with fine cuts because it allows me to integrate details and highlights in my rugs. This rug is hooked in three cuts. I included the constellation of Nick's birth sign, Gemini, in the upper right corner of the sky. The Big Dipper is over his other shoulder because it contains the North Star, a guiding star. I dyed nine values of blue to work with for this rug. I chose blue as the monochromatic color scheme because it was Nick's favorite color when he was a little boy.

All of these elements came together as part of his portrait, making it uniquely his. Creating rugs that include special elements is the fun part for me. Designing and hooking rugs allow me to express my feelings and ideas while giving me opportunities to explore color, texture, and creativity. I plan to give this rug to Nick after it's made its rounds in the rug hooking world where I teach. He loves it, and I'm glad I was able to capture the spirit and personality of a really special young man.

Nick@Night, 26" x 21", #3-cut hand-dyed wool on cotton linen.
Designed and hooked by Donna Hrkman, Dayton, Ohio, 2016. DAN HRKMAN

Donna Hrkman
Dayton, Ohio

Donna is a fine artist, rug hooker, designer, teacher, and member of ATHA. Nick@Night was exhibited at the Sauder Village rug show in August 2016 and was featured in the Jan/Feb 2017 issue of Rug Hooking *magazine. This is her tenth appearance in Celebration.*

Unique and exceptional! Superimposing a portrait on landscape is amazing artistry! Shading of hair and skin phenomenal; beautiful execution.

Ooh La La!

Our granddaughter, Peyton, visited France with her mother, Erika. Peyton fell in love with a blue beret and had to have it, and her mom, an excellent photographer, captured the moment perfectly. I saved many of their pictures from the trip, but I kept coming back to this particular one because of the "ooh la la" factor and Peyton's expressive blue eyes.

At Sauder Village, I had the opportunity to work with Donna Hrkman, so I selected Peyton with her beret as my next project. Donna and I worked extensively on the facial shading values. Next, we selected and designed a "wallpaper" background that complemented the portrait without overwhelming it with the greens and blues. Classes with Judy Carter really paid off because completing Peyton's eyes and hair

was easier than expected. Techniques I learned in Judy's "animals" class made using "as-is" wool for Peyton's hair a forgone conclusion, and she even helped me select the wool for the hair. In addition to Donna and Judy, Carol Kassera worked with me on shading Peyton's face. Her recommendations made a dramatic impact without excessive change.

Because the rug is adapted from a photo, the colors were set except for the background. I experimented with dip-dyeing wool to get the color values right, but it still took a lot of "tweaking" on the beret before I was satisfied. I learned a lot about shading and the influence of the direction of light on the rug. I kept trying different shades of blue and eventually got the look I wanted.

I think of myself and the women in my family as pioneer women. We're from

Minnesota where you can't always get to a store, so you learn to grow it, cook it, or make it! This hands-on approach led to all the arts I enjoy, including spinning, weaving, sewing, knitting, crocheting, cross-stitching, needle felting, and more. I like working with fiber, and it keeps my hands busy.

Lenny Feenan pushed me into my first attempt at portraiture, a piece called *Peyton and Ollie,* which features Peyton with her Great Dane, Ollie, in Scooby Doo hats to celebrate Ollie's birthday. Ollie and Peyton (and Scooby Doo!) presented many challenges, but Judy helped me a lot, and I was very happy with the final product. While I have hooked rugs that are not portraits, the portrait projects continue to challenge and reward me, and I look forward to creating my next project.

Ooh La La!, 17" x 20", #3- and #4-cut hand-dyed and as-is wool on rug warp. Adapted with permission from a photograph by Erika Page and hooked by Jannelle Kluch, Mazon, Illinois, 2016. LORI CORA

Jannelle Kluch
Mazon, Illinois

Jannelle was introduced to rug hooking in the 1990s but didn't fully commit until she and her friends visited Salt Box Primitive Woolens for a craft day. She is a member of the Foxy Lady Rug Hookers Guild and ATHA. This is her first appearance in Celebration.

In The Judges' Eyes

Well-done portrait with an appealing expression; eyelashes are captivating! The blues enhance each other.

Plane & Dog Team: 1931 Newfoundland Stamp

The Rug Hooking Guild of Newfoundland and Labrador had planned an exhibit containing hooked mats of Newfoundland stamps. This is the second of two that I hooked for the exhibit; it was added late to the collection. Both mats were Air Mail stamps in recognition of my heritage growing up in Gander, an airport town that served as an international refueling location for flights through World War II and many years beyond.

The stamp mat was hooked mostly with Dorr wool in value swatches, my favorite for work done with #3 cut. Several other samples of textures, however, were added to help create details in the dogs. Roving was used where the propeller is spinning to show air movement while black fishing line

was attached to provide a more convincing harness for the dog team.

These particular stamps were monochromatic, and although they were issued in several colors, I decided to use different shades of brown. I had registered for a class called "Monochromatic with a Difference," taught by Doris Norman, which helped me discover more ways to vary the color. I added a bit of orange to the plan, and the dogs have been hooked in part with textures that contain small flecks of color.

The treeline was so difficult to imagine initially since it was hooked with short wool strips. It wasn't until it was complete that I could actually see how closely it resembled the stamp. The dogs were the most challenging. They were very small, and I wanted to be able to see their tongues, ears,

paws, and tails. The dogs at the forefront were sculpted to help add a bit of dimension, and I wound up pulling out the harness, which I had originally hooked, to add fishing line.

I bought a Cheticamp trivet kit in the mid-1970s but didn't actually hook it until the early 1990s. After I retired, I took a class with the Newfoundland Guild and made my next mat in 2004. I've been hooking ever since! Rug hooking is an extension to other crafts I've been doing all of my life. I have always done a variety of crafts, mostly with textiles. Cross-stitching, sewing, and quilting have been the mainstays, but I've dabbled in many other crafts. Rug hooking allows me more freedom to explore color and design while allowing me to combine many techniques and fibers.

Plane & Dog Team: 1931 Newfoundland Stamp, 17½" x 20½", #3-cut hand-dyed and as-is wool, roving, and fishing line on linen. Adapted from a postage stamp by A.B. Perlin and hooked by Dianne Warren, St. John's, Newfoundland and Labrador, Canada, 2015.

Dianne Warren
St. John's, Newfoundland and Labrador, Canada

Dianne is a retired computer system analyst and project leader and currently operates a home-based rug hooking supplies business. She's a member of the Rug Hooking Guilds of Newfoundland and Labrador and Nova Scotia as well as TIGHR. This is her third appearance in Celebration.

Terrific! The details are riveting; the small details of the sled and dogs are well done; good use of texture in this monochromatic adaptation.

Shadow

I first saw Heather Haughn's photography when her mother forwarded this photo along with several others to me over Facebook. She thought they'd be of interest, and as soon as I saw this photo, I knew I wanted to hook it.

I started with the eyes, then the nose, and the wolf quickly came to life. The ears and mouth added dimension, and the long fur allowed me to proceed quickly with this piece. For the body, I hooked the light areas first, then the shadows, then filled in between the lights and the darks. This contrast also added dimension, particularly between the head and the body. The wispy hairs along the top of the head and body were hooked with many wools in different lengths to add realism.

I love to work with textured wools, and they were perfect for this project. Textured wool gives me the slight variations in color and value that I see in the photo. They allow me to blend the colors while creating highlights and shadows. The darker parts of the wool were clustered in areas to give the impression of depth and shadows while I kept the lighter part of the wool close to the wolf to ensure he remained a clear focal point. Most of the

wool I used was as-is, but I used penny-dyed wool for the whites. Penny dyeing dulls the bright shine of white wool and creates subtle shadows when hooked.

I finished the rug by zigzagging the edge, wrapping the edge over the cording, basting it in place, and then whipping the edge with wool yarn while adding the rug tape. Then the other edge of the rug tape was hand sewn into place before adding a label.

There were so many things I loved about this rug, but I especially loved the distant look in the eyes, how the nose was highlighted and the way the textured wool blends into the fur above it, and that fluffy neck. It makes me want to run my hands through that thick fur! I named the piece *Shadow* after doing research on names that mean "wolf."

I took a beginner class in rug hooking 24 years ago and have been hooking ever since. (In fact, this rug was the 126th rug I've ever hooked.) Rug hooking allows me to be creative and push the limits to see what I can do. I am always looking for the next project, the next challenge. I love experimenting to see if I can add more details and more realism.

Judy Carter
Willow Street, Pennsylvania

Judy is a Master Artisan with the Pennsylvania Guild of Craftsmen and is an accredited McGown teacher. She is also the author of Hooking Animals: How to Bring Animals to Life in Wool Rugs. *This is her fourteenth appearance in* Celebration.

Shadow, 21" x 21", #3- and #4-cut hand-dyed and as-is wool on rug warp. Adapted with permission from a photograph by Heather Haughn Photography and hooked by Judy Carter, Willow Street, Pennsylvania, 2016.

Exceptional animal portrait; great details with limited colors; his eyes seek you out; amazing piece in every way!

Two Birds Together

The inspiration for this rug came from a hand-carved antique wooden box. I decided to do a mirror look with a Fraktur design peacock. I used #4 cuts to outline the whole design to enhance the Fraktur look and help the colors to pop. I filled in the design with #6 cuts and then used #8 cuts for the background. The background is comprised of two colors: off-bolt oatmeal and hand-dyed soft green sage. I intertwined the colors while I hooked to create a marbled effect. The border originally had a leaf design repeated on the top and bottom; however, in the process of hooking I changed to bring in elements of the birds.

I seldom use blue as a main color, but I was really drawn to the particular blue I used for the birds. From there, I started choosing wools that coordinated well with that focal blue. I wanted the background to be soft to allow the birds and brighter elements to shine through. I still, however, wanted to achieve movement in the background, so I wove together the oatmeal and sage colors. While I don't usually outline my rugs, I wanted the design to pop and take on that Fraktur style.

My biggest challenge came partway through hooking when I changed the two borders closest to the birds. I had to redraw something and then try to get both sides of the pattern even when part of the rug had already been hooked! I've found myself doing this more and more when hooking different patterns, but the final product makes it worth the effort.

I was first introduced to hooked rugs after I saw them at a store in Denver in 1998. It was love at first sight. I knew I wanted to learn this art for myself, but it was another ten years before I was finally able to pursue it. I had moved to Utah and asked the owner of a local quilt shop if she knew any rug hookers, and after my first lesson, I was smitten.

I've been creating art since I was small—it seemed like I always had to be doing something with my hands. I love rug hooking because it's forgiving with mistakes or changes. You can be creative with the materials you choose, and different hooking and cutting techniques can change the entire look of a piece. The possibilities are endless.

Tonia McKibben
Wellsville, Utah

Tonia was on the original board for the Utah Rug and Fiber Guild when it was established and currently serves as the guild's vice president. This is her first appearance in Celebration.

Two Birds Together, 53" x 27", #4-, #6- and #8-cut hand-dyed and as-is wool on linen. Adapted from an 18th century wooden carved box and hooked by Tonia McKibben, Wellsville, Utah, 2016.
ANNE-MARIE LITTENBERG

In The Judges' Eyes

Good placement of colors; outstanding colors and composition.

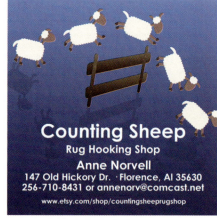

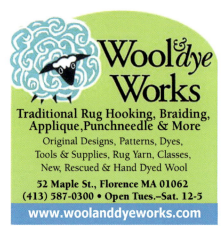

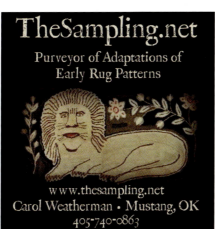
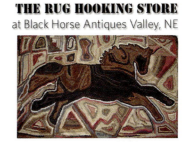

Fraktur Blessings

In 2009, I was asked to teach a class at my local ATHA chapter that would be about special stitches and Pennsylvania Dutch patterns. I designed several rug patterns for the class, and this was one of them. While no one chose this pattern at that class, I've had several students choose it for other classes I've taught. When our ATHA chapter invited Monika Jones to teach a workshop in 2015, I decided this pattern might be the perfect project to work on with her.

I love blue and gold; when autumn leaves turn yellow and the sky is blue with big, puffy clouds, it makes my heart sing! Letting that be my starting place, I bought some gray textured wool; a rich, burnt orange-red plaid; and three gold textured wools from Monika's offerings. I brought some of my own recycled wool along with some of my own favorite blue spot-dyed wool. The gray, acting as a cool neutral color, worked perfectly in the background. I like to keep light gray spots on hand for my students and customers, so I combined three of my own light gray spots with Monika's gray plaid for a mottled background.

My mother, Emma Webber, always used recycled materials with her rugs. As a teacher, I decided to offer my students new quality wool. I see the value in both recycled and new wools and like to use both in my own projects. I planned to "outline and fill" this project, one of my favorite rug hooking techniques, and started off with a recycled plaid outlining. Monika works with textured wools that she throws a little dye on to give it an aged and weathered look, like a patina.

I chose some of her wool to experience her influence.

There isn't one particular section that I like more than any other; it's a simple piece and has a nice flow. I love the gold textured outline that's so graphic. I like echoing the motifs with a variety of the textures in the background. I like the smidgen of dirty red plaid, the three different blues, and the careful distribution of yellow and gold. The Fraktur symbolism offers peace, harmony, good luck, good fortune, and love.

My mother, Emma, hooked and braided rugs all of my life. When a new ATHA chapter started up in Sonoma County in 1996, Emma was invited to attend. We decided it was time for me to start hooking, and we'd have some great adventures together. I've been hooking ever since.

Laura Pierce
Petaluma, California

Laura is a Jill-of-many-trades but currently teaches the art and craft of rug hooking. Her Celebration-winning rug, Emmy, was on the cover of the June/July/August 2009 issue of Rug Hooking *magazine. This is her seventh appearance in* Celebration.

In The Judges' Eyes

Lovely colors; nice background movement; nice interplay of colors; execution and color plan all deserve mention.

Fraktur Blessings, 20" x 36", #5- and #8-cut hand-dyed, recycled, and as-is textures on linen.
Designed and hooked by Laura Pierce, Petaluma, California, 2015.

New Bedford Hearth Rug

I love whales. I bought this Edyth O'Neill's pattern on a hook-in "sale" table. Someone else had thought it was for them, but really, it was for me! Sometimes rugs germinate—you think about them but aren't quite ready to hook them. Last year, when I was going to a hook-in where I was supposed to finish a UFO, I decided to take the whale and some wool I had collected for it instead.

I knew the whale needed to be the focus, so I chose three neutrals to create him. To help him stand out, I chose a darker color for the background that still had touches of color. I chose to hook the paisley-style waves in different shades of blue. I used a textured wool to separate the background and the border, which was yet another dark wool with some red in it to play off the scallop separation. Using dark wools that had color in them helped to give the rug movement and life. I finished the rug by using a wool blanket binding.

When making this rug, I learned how much I love primitive-style rugs. Much like a painting, you direct the message your rug is sending by your choices.

My friend, Judy Glenn, and I went to a rug camp in Arkansas without having ever pulled a loop. In fact, I had never seen a hooked rug at this point. My teacher was Sally Kallin and, before I ever pulled a loop, I was hooked. I'm a folk art painter, a simple knitter, and an aspiring wool applique student, but I absolutely adore rug hooking. I love the people I get to meet, the creativity of others, the opportunities to learn new ways to express myself, and in the end, you have a new favorite rug. That is, until you hook the next one!

I wish I had discovered rug hooking earlier in my life. There are so many patterns that I want to hook with all of this beautiful wool in my stash. I think I may need to find a way to clone myself to get through it all.

Sondra M. Ives
Houston, Texas

Sondra is retired from the University of Texas Medical School at Houston where she was the Director of Admissions and Alumni Affairs. She's a member of The Stash Sisters (Region 9) chapter of ATHA. This is her first appearance in Celebration.

In The Judges' Eyes

Directional hooking skillful and effective, especially in whale's head; well done.

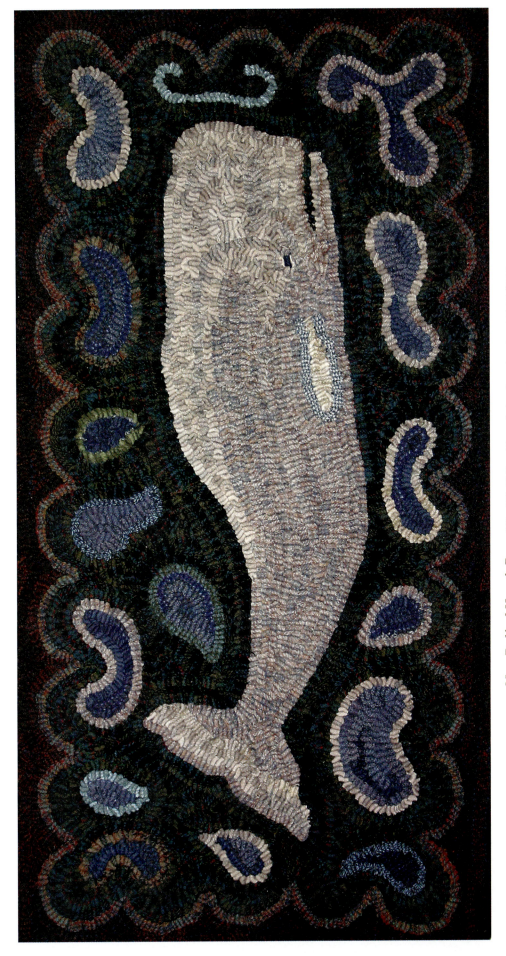

New Bedford Hearth Rug, 42" x 23", #9.5-cut hand-dyed and as-is wool on linen.
Designed by Edyth O'Neill and hooked by Sondra M. Ives, Houston, Texas, 2016. KRISTI ROBERTS

October Log Cabin

I've long been attracted to the endless graphic possibilities that the "log cabin" concept presents. I've hooked on that theme many times, having done rugs, pillows, chair pads, and small mats in that style. There are limitless patterns to create and colors to juxtapose in just a simple diagonally divided block, which satisfies my desires to maintain structure while playing with colors and space. A recent exhibition at the Museum of American Folk Art in New York City featured old-fashioned log cabin designs made from recycled office paper and supplies, old exposed photographic film, and many other recycled materials. It made me realize that I am far from alone in my fascination with this design.

I'm pretty traditional when it comes to choosing materials because I feel strongly that the rugs I make are to be both functional and enjoyable. Generally, that means they live on the floor, so I can't have anything fragile and use very few novelty embellishments (although I love silk and velvet). I do love a bit of sparkle though, so I'm happy when I find wool with glitter woven in. If you look carefully, you can find a bit of that in *October Log Cabin*.

Finding success with log cabin designs is all about the right combinations of color. Because I began knowing that I wanted the leaves to drift down onto the rug and then really "pop," I decided to put them against very light "squares." I had also recently seen a rug where some of the motifs were all in creams and whites, and I was taken with how they just jumped off the surface. So after studying my wall of wool, I decided to challenge myself to see if I could make black and purple exciting as opposed to funereal. The bright leaves and the traditional red chimneys and border line worked well for that.

This rug reminded me how balance and design are much more important than they appear. It's not something the viewer should have to think about; they should be visually satisfied without thinking about why. The placement of those leaves may seem random (like it should!), but I moved the templates around many, many times before I traced them.

Having been in the arts and antiques field my whole career, I had admired antique hooked rugs and always wanted to learn how to make them. I was so lucky to find Nancy McClennen and Claire de Roos in Binghamton, New York, along with a McGown guild. They put a hook in my hand, and I've never looked back.

Kathleen Harwood
South Hadley, Massachusetts

Kathleen is a consultant, appraiser, and writer in the field of fine arts and is best known as an appraiser on PBS's Antiques Roadshow. She's a member of the Green Mountain Guild in Vermont and has participated in hooking communities in the Berkshires, New York state, and Brattleboro, Vermont. This is her fifth appearance in Celebration.

In The Judges' Eyes

Multiple borders form a perfect frame; fabulous color choices and depth, nicely done.

October Log Cabin, 30½" x 42¼", #4- to 8-cut hand-dyed and as-is wool on linen.
Designed and hooked by Kathleen Harwood, South Hadley, Massachusetts, 2016. VAN ZANDBERGEN PHOTOGRAPHY

Sue's Star & Pennies Room Rug

leave that part of the process to the experts. Instead, I enjoy the "hunt" for the perfect colored wool.

The large center star is a real stunner with the aqua boucle and orange-striped wool adding a lot to its appeal. To make the interior background more interesting, it was broken up into subsections by drawing curvy swaths. Each section had one wool, so each could be seen individually. All of the wools were close in value but not the same dye or bolt of wool. It made the background much more interesting for me to hook and more visually appealing.

For me, the most challenging part of any rug is the color planning. You have to consider how the colors will play off each other within a section as well as in the piece as a whole. Even picking colors for the leaves that complement each other takes careful consideration.

With this rug, I learned that the look of shading can be accomplished by using just a few wools. Each leaf consists of three wools—one for the stem and veins and two others for the leaf itself.

I first became interested in rug hooking when I took a beginner class in 2002. Although I struggled during the class, I continued hooking after it was over because I love the look of hand-hooked rugs. While I also knit and quilt and enjoy wool appliqué, I enjoy rug hooking because I find pulling loops very relaxing.

I continue to be inspired by rugs hooked by others. I love all styles of hooking but particularly embrace the primitive style. The rug hooking community is filled with such talented, interesting, and generous people who I am lucky to learn from and call my friends.

I first saw an oval version of this pattern designed by Cathy Stephan called *Gloria's Oval*. I asked Cathy to redesign it for me as a rectangle. She added the small stars to the corners, and I fell in love with the pattern that she had designed and named in my honor. It's the largest rug I have hooked so far.

Textured wools are my favorite, and I used many different types to add visual interest to the rug. I also love autumn colors, so I chose the tomato red background for the interior rug to really give it a splash of color. I don't dye my own wool. I have taken just enough dye classes to appreciate all of the work involved in dyeing wools but I

Susan G. Dollhopf
Neenah, Wisconsin

Susan is a commercial insurance agent. Sue's Star & Pennies Room Rug won third place at the September 2016 hook-in sponsored by Heart of Wisconsin Rug Hooking Guild. This is her first appearance in Celebration.

In The Judges' Eyes

Admirable color choices; gorgeous; great use of textures; love the red background.

Sue's Star & Pennies Room Rug, 42" x 75", #8.5-cut wool on linen. Designed by Cathy Stephan of Red Barn Rugs and hooked by Susan G. Dollhopf, Neenah, Wisconsin, 2016. DEAN DOERSCH

Ancient Egypt, 38" x 54", #3-cut dyed wool on rug warp.
Designed and hooked by Tanya Knodel, Sudbury, Ontario, Canada, 2016.

Artsy Runner, 86" x 46", #4 to 8-cut hand-dyed wool on linen.
Designed and hooked by Sharon A. Smith, Walnut Creek, California, 2016.

Carnival Paws, 45" x 27", traditional proddy rug made with hand-torn ½" wool selvedges on primitive linen. Designed and hooked by Gene Shepherd, Anaheim, California, 2015.

Diamond, 18" x 18", #2- to 6-cut hand-dyed and as-is wool and cotton yarn on suiting boucle. Designed and hooked by Capri Boyle Jones, Navarre, Florida, 2016.

Flower Festival, 45" x 32", #4- to 6-cut hand-dyed and as-is wool on linen.
Designed and hooked by Kelly Kanyok, Independence, Ohio, 2016. BETH MOORE

Mother and Child, 17½" x 14½", #4-cut
hand-dyed wool on linen. Adapted from
The Three Ages of Women by Gustav Klimt
and hooked by Val Flannigan, Kelowna,
British Columbia, Canada, 2016. GRAEME
FLANNIGAN

Rick Rack, 51" x 34", #9- and #9.5-cut new and scrap wool on linen. Designed by Nancy Parcels and hooked by Sheri Jane Bennett, Chattanooga, Tennessee, 2016. JESSIE LANGSTON

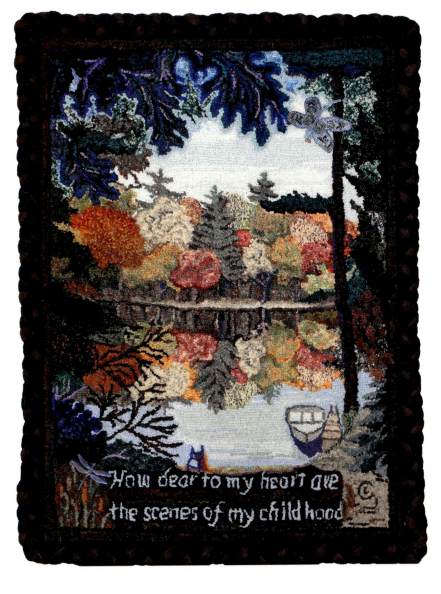

Scenes of My Childhood, 20" x 26", #3-cut wool, novelty yarns, tie tacks, beads, needle felting, and creative stitches on linen. Designed and hooked by Grace Collette, Raymond, New Hampshire, 2016.

Snakes and Ladders, 31" x 31", #3- to 6-cut hand-dyed and recycled wool on linen. Designed and hooked by Linda Stockford, Wickham, New Brunswick, Canada, 2016.

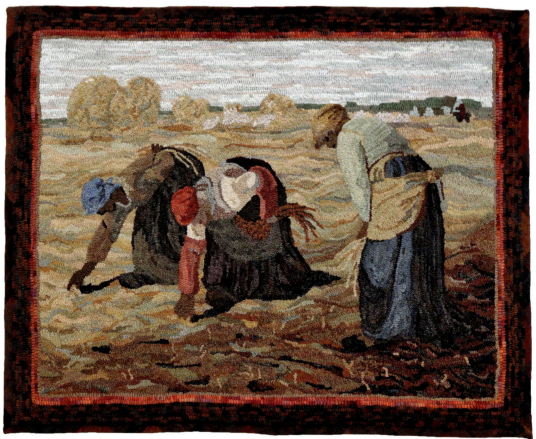

The Gleaners, 54" x 42", #8- and 8.5-cut wool on linen. Adapted by Cathy Stephan from a painting by Jean-Francois Millet. Hooked by Marilyn Denning, Burlington, Wisconsin, 2016.

The Hookery, 36" x 24", #4- and #5-cut hand-dyed and as-is wool on linen.
Designed and hooked by Linda Bell, Hiawassee, Georgia, 2015. SHAWNTA SHOOK

Treasure Spots, 32½" x 23", #3- to 5-cut hand-dyed and as-is wool on linen. Designed by Akiko Nishi &
Chizuko Hayami and hooked by Chizuko Hayami, Setagayaku, Japan, 2016. JUN KONTA

Turkey!, 37" x 30", #3- to 5-cut hand-dyed and as-is wool on cotton rug warp.
Designed and hooked by John Leonard, Wilmington, North Carolina, 2016. MATT BORN

Zeus and Aimie Memory Rug, 32" x 21", #4-cut wool on rug warp. Pattern drawn by Leonard Feenan from
a photograph by Patricia Cassidy and hooked by Patricia Cassidy, Sandusky, Ohio, 2016.

Ad Index

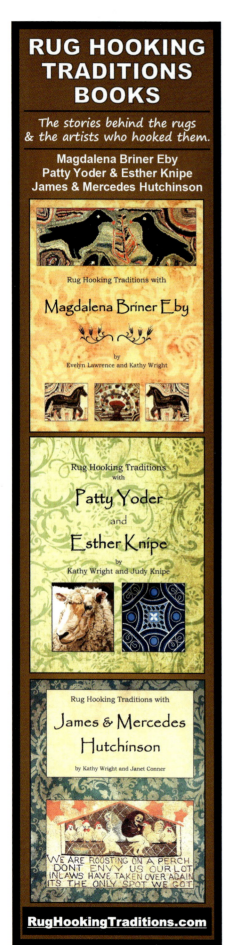